CREATING A TRADITIONAL
ELK CAMP

A ROCKY MOUNTAIN ELK FOUNDATION BOOK

CREATING A TRADITIONAL ELK CAMP

Where the Heart of the Hunt Is Found

Jack Ballard

THE LYONS PRESS

Guilford, Connecticut

AN IMPRINT OF THE GLOBE PEQUOT PRESS

The Lyons Press is an imprint of The Globe Pequot Press

10 9 8 7 6 5 4 3 2 1

Printed in the United States of America

ISBN-13: 978-1-59228-821-2
ISBN-10: 1-59228-821-9

Library of Congress Cataloging-in-Publication Data is available on file.

DEDICATION

This book is dedicated to the Ballard brothers: George Dudley, Jr., Jack, and Tom. George, my father, who gave me life. Jack, my uncle, who lent me his good name and many hours' laughter. And Tom, who is the living patriarch and soul of our family elk camp.

CONTENTS

ACKNOWLEDGMENTS

This work bears my name, but many others share equal credit for its words. My uncle, Tom, has taught me more about elk hunting and woodcraft than he will ever realize. Leroy, my older brother, is the best big-game hunter I know. We've pitched many tents together, each adventure yielding more knowledge of hunting and camping in elk country.

Priscilla Cunningham of Yellowstone Baptist College taught me to write. Her merciful evaluation of my freshman prose and her encouragement at several key junctures in my development as a writer have enabled me to make a living with words.

Producing photos to illustrate this text became a major challenge, even though I view myself as much a photographer as a writer. The technical and creative abilities of my friend Brad Johnson are behind most of the images.

Fran, my wife, also deserves much credit. She is my best editor and best friend.

Finally, I am infinitely indebted to the Creator of the eternal blue sky whose breath stirs life in all things, wild and human. May we respect the Earth and one another as His handiwork.

PREFACE

In one sense, the title of this book is misleading, because camps of the type described here have applications far beyond elk hunting. I've pitched my wall tent in the Black Hills of South Dakota while hunting whitetail deer. My wife, two sons of preschool age, and I have camped in Montana's Beartooth Mountains in the dead of winter in a wall tent to sled, ski, and revel in the wild solitude. We've even made "elk camp" in the backyard—just last weekend my four-year-old daughter hosted two bright-eyed friends and her older brothers in a wall-tent sleepover.

The attractions of a traditional elk camp are comfort and portability. Sure, you can hunt from a backpacker's tent, as I've done many times, but if the temperature plummets below zero and you awaken to six inches of snow on the ground, you're not likely to stay long at the game. By contrast, such conditions just make for finer hunting and happier camping when there's a fire crackling in the wood stove of a wall tent.

Don't like the area you're hunting? If you've booked a room in a local motel, you can't hook your pickup to the front desk and drag your accommodations to the next drainage. With a traditional elk camp, though, you're free to move pretty much wherever your heart desires.

The information in this book is a collection of lore gleaned from my family's fifty-plus years of experience in an elk camp near the headwaters of the Ruby River in southwest Montana. This is how we do it. That's not to say it's the only way or necessarily the best way. But I believe you'll find enough information to point you in the right direction—and a few good stories to brighten the way.

FOREWORD

from the Rocky Mountain Elk Foundation

Part of the mystique of elk and elk hunting comes from the fundamentally *large* nature of the experience: Big cagey animals. Big beguiling country. Big weather. Big excitement. And big camps. An extended backcountry elk-hunt party can seem almost like an expeditionary force, armed and mounted. The logistics can be overwhelming. This book is the answer. Jack Ballard offers elk hunters—and anyone else contemplating a prolonged stay in wild country—a handbook for maximizing ease, comfort, and success.

"Proper planning prevents poor performance" might be Ballard's motto.

The Rocky Mountain Elk Foundation is proud to partner with The Lyons Press in producing an informative and well-written resource for our members, and for all who have known, or may come to know, the pleasures of a good camp. All the essential ingredients of a traditional elk hunting party are here. You can almost see, smell, hear, and feel the heavy canvas, wood heat and woodsmoke, lantern light, good food, and good company.

Ballard's voice is clearly one of both experience and expertise. His economy of words matches the economy of effort that his book will bring to outdoorsmen and women seeking the optimal outdoor experience—the keys to a camp of comfort, safety, and confidence.

This is an essential book for a very rare and special breed of person: the tent-camp elk hunter. Wall tents, wood stoves, and gas lanterns—the classic camp for the classic elk hunt. This title is destined to be a classic on the subject—definitive, comprehensive, comprehensible, and sure to be a welcome gift and resource for elk hunters, those new to camp, and those who have traversed many miles in search of a trophy bull. This book will help you appreciate a good camp not only for the comfort it may provide, but also for the skill, wisdom, logic, and love of it.

J. Dart
President
Rocky Mountain Elk Foundation

— 1 —

WALL TENTS AND ACCESSORIES

A half-mile before cresting the rise that opens into a broad, long clearing, I catch a whiff of smoke in the twisting thermals that curl down the trail I'm ascending. The smoke, I know, is rising lazily from stovepipes poking from the tents that house my family's elk camp.

The sun disappeared nearly an hour ago, but I haven't reached for my flashlight until now—I know this trail well enough to navigate in the dim light of the fading glow on the western horizon. Casting the beam of my light here and there, I look for the smoke. The smell is there, distinct and sharp in the crisp evening air. But try as I might, I can't see the hazy-blue emissions creating the odor.

My pace quickens. The scent of the smoke has brought to mind an enticing picture of what lies ahead. In ten minutes I'll be at camp in the meadow. I'll pull back the tent flap and leave behind the intensifying chill for an atmosphere as warm and inviting as my living room back home. From a warm seat, I'll pull my feet from damp boots and turn my toes toward the wood stove in the corner. Some kind soul will succor me with a cup of steaming cocoa, or a plum glass of merlot. Then I'll regale my companions with a tale of the day's hunt. Afterward we'll eat dinner. Ending the evening with a rousing match of cribbage or a mellow sojourn with a book, I'll nestle into a cozy bed of flannel and fall fast asleep.

The structure that makes such comfort possible at an 8,000-foot elevation, deep in the mountains of southwestern Montana, is a canvas wall tent. Some of the finest nights of my life have passed within such shelters. Fond memories, a few reaching nearly three decades into the recesses of my mind, come to consciousness when I catch the pungent odor of treated canvas: images of my deceased father and uncle laughing, hunting, or lounging about camp.

Other pictures come to mind as well. I remember crawling into my old cotton sleeping bag after a long survey of the thousand pinpricks of light flickering in the Milky Way overhead. At dawn, I poked my head from the same tent to behold new wonders in the heavens—huge, weaving snowflakes descending purposefully from a gray ceiling. But the change in weather didn't chase us from the mountains. Snug behind sturdy walls of twelve-ounce canvas, I just poked an extra log in the wood stove after eating breakfast, and then went back to bed. Others played cards in the cook tent until the snow let up enough for hunting.

The author's elk camp, just like his father's elk camp.

Wall tents are the heart of a traditional elk-hunting camp for good reason. They're sturdier than nylon camping tents. And properly pitched, they'll shrug off a heavy snow load that would collapse a nylon tent supported by thin aluminum poles. What's more, nearly all wall tents are designed and constructed with a heating source in mind. They safely accommodate a woodburning stove, and the canvas provides a surprising degree of insulation. Long before recreational elk hunters latched onto wall tents for their camps, prospectors, settlers, and soldiers passed entire winters behind canvas.

Size

Choosing the size and style of a tent (or tents) to fit your crew is the first step in creating a camp.

How large a tent will you need to lodge your group? Some manufacturers advertise various tents as suitable for a specified number of individuals—four people, six people, and so on. Unfortunately, many of these ratings are hopelessly optimistic. Will a ten-by-ten-foot tent really handle four hunters, as I once saw advertised? Maybe if they're very good friends. But if they spend much time pinched together in a tent that size, I'll guarantee that they won't be such bosom buddies when they break camp. Do the math. A ten-by-ten-foot tent gives each fellow five square feet of space inside, with no extra area for cooking or a heating stove—not my idea of a good time.

Rather than relying on the manufacturer's rating or the recommendations of an acquaintance, I suggest you take a more direct approach. On a garage floor or driveway, arrange your gear (or sketch mock-ups of it in chalk) as you anticipate it being organized in the tent. Experiment with different arrangements. Once you've arrived at a desired configuration, measure the outer dimensions, adding about six inches on each side for clearance along the sidewalls of the tent. This is the tent size you require.

However, there's one other size consideration before you make a purchase. A tent advertised as twelve by fourteen feet may not actually be that large. The true dimensions can vary considerably depending on whether the figure represents the size of the canvas before being folded and stitched along corners and seams or the actual finished size of the tent. Ascertain the actual dimensions of the tent before you buy to make sure you don't lose needed space to canvas gobbled up in the tent-construction process.

Tents also vary in wall height. Essentially, wall height determines the portion of the tent that can be used comfortably. Unless you enjoy impersonating the hunchback of Notre Dame in your camp, make sure to opt for sufficiently high sidewalls. Most manufacturers now sew tents with five-foot sidewalls as the standard dimension, which allows hunters to utilize the entire tent without a lot of bending over. Tents with three- or four-foot sidewalls may be cheaper, but they greatly restrict the area that can be navigated. Some smaller tents designed primarily for backcountry or spike camps have six-foot sidewalls that allow an average-sized person to walk erect in the entire tent. If you're on the shorter side, like me, you might be tempted to save a little money by buying a tent with lower sidewalls. However, when the time comes to load meat on a mule or hang a lantern from the ridgepole, those tall guys are handy to have around. Think of their comfort along with your wallet. For general use, I highly recommend tents with five-foot sidewalls.

Features

Wall tents are most commonly made from treated, cotton canvas. The "treating" applied is typically a combined flame-retardant and moisture/mildew reducer. Canvas weight varies with the manufacturer. Heavier fabrics of comparable quality make the tent more durable, but may add so much extra weight that the tent is cumbersome for one or two people to handle. Ten-ounce treated canvas is commonly used for wall tents and is more than adequate for any do-it-yourself elk camp.

Recently, some companies began creating traditional wall tents with noncanvas materials or combining canvas and another material. Controlling weight is the most common goal for such innovations. A synthetic material on the sidewalls and end panels can reduce the weight of a tent by roughly 30 percent. Thus, the weight

An older tent with no sod cloth and canvas ties on the door flap. Note positioning of the chimney.

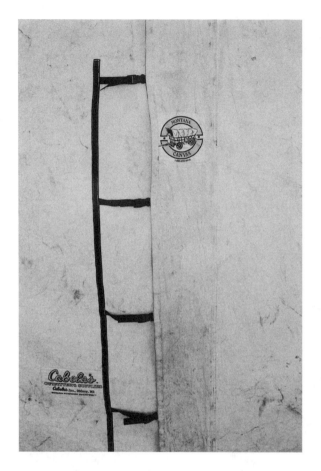

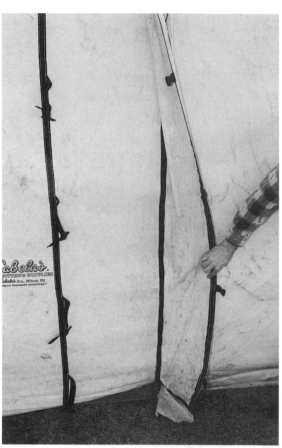

(Left) The outer tent flap held with plastic, quick-release buckles.

(Right) The zippered inner tent flap.

of a twelve-by-fourteen-foot canvas tent with five-foot sidewalls may drop from around seventy pounds to forty pounds or so if a lighter material is incorporated. For backcountry applications, the weight savings is definitely worth considering even though tents made partially or completely from synthetic materials are normally more costly than canvas tents.

In the past, the flaps (doors) of wall tents were made from overlapping sheets of canvas secured on the outside and inside with slender canvas ties. Some had stovepipe ports sewn into the tent while others had to be split on a seam so a removable metal jack

Sod cloth sewn to the bottom of a wall tent helps keep out drafts.

A zippered, screened window in a wall tent.

could be inserted for the stovepipe. Nowadays, heat-resistant rubber jacks that form an airtight seal around the stovepipe are the norm in tent construction. Most tents currently come from the manufacturer with a stove jack, although a few makers charge extra for them. Inner flaps are commonly held shut with heavy-duty zippers instead of ties, while click-together buckles and nylon webbing secure the outer flaps. A sod cloth—a strip of material sewn to the bottom of the walls of the tent—is now standard equipment on most wall tents as well. Soil can be heaped over the sod cloth to seal out drafts around the bottom of the tent. If you're considering the purchase of a tent lacking any of these "standard" features, its price should be reduced accordingly.

Additional features are generally sold as accessories and raise the price of the tent. For early season hunting, a zippered window that can be opened to help cool the tent is a worthwhile investment.

Even when there's snow on the ground, a window is handy when some absentminded campmate stokes too much wood in the stove and then leaves everyone else to endure the sauna.

It's also possible to purchase tents that have a door sewn in both ends or to have another door added to a tent you already own. Rather than buying two freestanding tents, some hunters just add an extension for cooking onto the tent they already own. With a door on each end of the tent, it's possible to directly enter or exit the sleeping or cooking areas. If your cook is a crabby fellow who doesn't appreciate hunters tramping through his kitchen, an additional door in the tent makes good sense.

Installing the floor in a wall tent is a lot like putting in a rug.

Floors and Flies

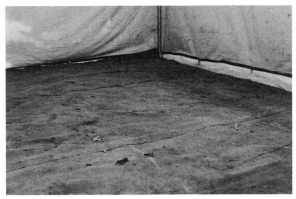

Flooring in a wall tent made with a canvas tarp.

Floors are available from most manufacturers too. Some offer permanent floors sewn right into the bottom of the tent, while others make removable floors that are cut and sewn to fit a particular tent and attached to the sidewalls with grommets or straps.

But do you really need a floor in a wall tent? My answer is an emphatic *yes*. A few days of foot traffic in and out of a tent will grind soil into a fine, dusty powder that winds up on everything. And if it rains or a snowstorm barrels in, a floor gives people a dry place to stand—if they have the sense to remove their wet boots by the door. Tent floors also protect grass and other plants from excessive damage.

Although manufactured floors fit nicely and are generally of high quality, they can add up to a couple hundred dollars to the price of your tent. Homemade floors are a more economical alternative. When a heavy canvas tarp I used as a trailer cover developed some small tears and holes a few years back, I designated it as a tent floor. It doesn't fit perfectly, but it covers the length of my tent and most of the width. We've also made floors from used military tarps at our family camp, as the stiff, weighty canvas keeps the floor from moving around underfoot.

Secure your tent so it is strong enough to withstand the weight of snow; you never know how much snow you'll get.

No matter what type of floor you choose, take care when arranging it around a wood stove. Cut or fold it so it remains a safe distance from the stove to avoid burning. An extra measure of caution should be taken when loading the stove or removing ashes: embers that wind up on a tent floor quickly burn through.

Another item that's sold separately but is an absolute necessity is a tent fly, a fabric covering placed over the top of the wall tent to shed water. Last season we pitched two tents at our camp. The cook tent was promptly covered with a fly, but the crew that pitched the sleeping tent (I wasn't a part of it, honest) figured they'd put the fly on the following day.

They didn't. Nor did they cover the tent the next day, or the next, or the next. But the weather was wonderful and it didn't matter—until the night before we broke camp. At midnight it started to rain. At 3 A.M. it turned to snow. At 5 A.M. I awoke suddenly. Droplets of water were splashing down on my forehead that couldn't have been more perfectly aimed by a master of the ancient art of water torture. My sleeping bag was also wet from the waist down, but my bladder mercifully full. The tent was obviously leaking, not me.

What to do? After a few moments' thought, I lit the lantern, stoked the stove, and awakened the slacker crew that couldn't find twenty minutes to throw the fly on the tent. By daylight our camp was nearly dismantled. Never before had we exited the mountains so early or quickly on the final day. Never again will slothful souls be allowed to eat until all the tents are covered.

Extend the fly over the sidewall for outside gear storage.

As with floors, most wall-tent manufacturers sell matching flies with their tents. Most are made of tough, high-quality waterproof fabric and designed with a port for the stovepipe that boasts a seal to keep moisture from seeping under the fly and onto the tent roof. But like custom floors, these flies are expensive, easily adding another $150 to the purchase price of your tent.

SIZING A RAINFLY

If you buy your own tarp or create a fly from other material, you'll have to figure out the correct size. Unless you can actually measure the tent, you'll have to take another approach. Think high school geometry was a worthless subject? Think again. If you know the length, width, and height (measured from the ridgepole to the ground) of the tent and the height of the sidewalls (dimensions commonly available from the manufacturer), it's simple to calculate the size of a well-fitting fly before purchasing the tent.

First, subtract the height of the sidewalls from the overall height. Then square this number. Divide the width of the tent by two. Square this number as well. Add the two squares, and find the square root of the sum. This square root is the length of one side of the roof measured from the eave to the peak. Double this figure, then add about four feet or more to allow the fly to overhang the sidewalls of the tent. This number is the required length of the fly. The width of the fly is the same as the length of the tent.

Confused? How about a quick example of the Pythagorean theorem in action. Suppose you buy a 12-by-14-foot tent with 5-foot sidewalls and a center height of 9 feet. Subtract the sidewalls from the height: 9 - 5 = 4. Squaring 4 feet yields 16 feet. Now divide the width by two: 12 ÷ 2 = 6. Squaring 6 feet yields 36 feet. Add the two squares: 16 + 36 = 52. The square root of 52 feet is roughly 7.2 feet. Doubling this figure yields 14.4 feet. Adding 4 feet for overhang leaves you with a length of 18.4 feet. And we already know that the length of the tent (width of the fly) is 14 feet. Thus, a 14-by-18-foot fly or one of similar dimensions will be ideal for your tent.

One of the most common alternatives to a custom fly are the lightweight, poly tarps sold at nearly any hardware store or home center. Poly tarps aren't nearly as durable as flies manufactured specifically for wall tents, but if they're tied securely and care is taken not to snag them on sharp objects, which will start a tear, such tarps will endure several seasons of casual use. Heavier, construction- or farm-grade tarps also make excellent flies that will endure for over a decade if used and stored properly. I've even seen

THE ULTIMATE STAKE

Not liking what we had, my Uncle Tom, a machinist, set out one year to create better stakes for our tents. The resulting invention wasn't beautiful, but it was very effective. In his shop, Tom cut 1/2-inch rebar into lengths of about 10 inches. He then cut one end from the links of a piece of chain with bolt cutters to create a bunch of U-shaped hooks. To each piece of rebar he welded one side of a hook with the points of the U facing downward. The result is a very strong stake with a secure rope hook that can be made for pennies—and one smug uncle.

tents covered with clear, heavy plastic. This may be low on durability, especially when it's windy and cold, but clear plastic allows plenty of natural light into the tent during the day and repels water.

No matter what type of fly you use, I'd strongly suggest that you extend it a couple of feet or more beyond the eaves of the tent. Not only does this keep dripping water or sliding snow away from the tent, it also provides a sheltered place to store items like chainsaws, packsaddles, axes, and other gear you don't want to cache inside.

Tent Stakes

You'll also need tent stakes to secure the tent to the ground. Some manufacturers supply stakes with their tents, others don't. Lightweight metal or plastic tent pegs intended for nylon camping tents are a poor choice for wall tents, which are much heavier and typically exposed to more extreme weather.

Heavy-duty stakes are available from some outdoor retail stores and well-stocked mail-order companies like Cabela's. These are usually formed from a tapered section of lightweight angle iron and sport a hook for attaching ropes to the peg. The hook can also be inserted in the grommets at the bottom of the sidewall if your tent is so equipped, making it possible to stake the sidewall without attaching rope loops to the grommets.

While these stakes are vastly superior to the cheapies, they can still buckle when driven against a rock or into hard ground and

may twist or bend under heavy use. Railroad spikes, used or new, make durable tent stakes, but in soft or sandy soil they're not long enough to get a good "bite" in the ground. Heavy nails (spikes) in the 10-inch range with flat washers to keep the ropes from slipping off make excellent stakes in hard ground for a tent's guylines, but they don't work as well for staking the tent bottom unless a loop of rope or webbing is attached to each grommet.

My best recommendation on tent stakes is to acquire a variety, then mix and match to meet the ground conditions where you pitch the tent. And take a few extras in case some are lost or damaged. If you accidentally drive a stake into the root of a lodge pole pine, you won't have to worry about it being loosened by wind or weather, but you won't get it back either.

With a tent, fly, and stakes on hand, you're almost ready to hit the mountains.

A large spike (nail) with a washer used as tent stake.

– 2 –

SELECTING A CAMPSITE

The sun set as we motored up the Ruby River Road. Creeping shadows darkened the benches above the river, tarnishing the silver hues of sage. Soon they engulfed aspen groves in the creek bottoms and blackened pines on the flanks of the mountains. At last they conquered the peaks themselves, bringing to end the final, brilliant show of light on the crags.

"How much longer we drivin'?" Dave asked.

"About another five miles on this road and then another hour or so up the bench road into camp," I replied.

"How's our camp going to go up in the dark?" he said.

Dave had never been to elk camp. In fact, he'd never been hunting at all. But I knew he'd love the homey solitude of a wall tent and the challenge of slinking around the timber attempting to outwit a dark-maned bull. We'd shared many hiking and fishing trips in the course of our friendship and I was especially enthused about this hunt.

"We'll just leave the headlights on, pull the poles out of the timber, and have the tent set up in an hour," I responded confidently. "This ain't the first time I've put up a camp in the dark."

Just off the main road we hit mud, the product of snow that had melted into the twin tire tracks leading up the mountain. We chained up the front end of the old Jeep Wagoneer and locked the transfer case in low. Just before Beaver Creek, on a shaded bend where the ruts get deep and treacherous, the headlights revealed standing water in the track ahead. Out came another set of chains for the rear tires.

We churned ahead while I continually assured Dave that the worst would be over in a quarter-mile. Actually, the worst hit much sooner.

Within a hundred feet we found ourselves high-centered on a rut in a brown sea of cold muck.

Slopping around, I finally got the front wheels jacked up and a few small logs wedged under the tires in the rut. Dave attached a come-a-long to the back bumper, then strung a length of tow rope to a tree. Foot by foot, we grappled back onto semi-solid ground.

By now it was obvious we weren't going farther up the road. Feebly we looked around for a place to camp at our current location. Searching for tent poles in the timber, in the dark, with a flashlight, is little fun under any conditions, but even less so with your pants and boots sodden with freezing muck.

We stayed at the job for a short time, then gave up, turned the Jeep back down the mountain and made the three-hour drive back to the family ranch where my surprised mother greeted us shortly after midnight.

Finding an ideal campsite and leaving yourself enough daylight to construct at least the basic elements of a camp are the first challenges of hunting in new territory. Even when heading to a known location, you should arrive well before dark. Had we hit the road just two hours earlier, Dave and I would have had time to put together a camp where the road became impassable.

Locating your camp in just the right spot can make the difference between a great and not-so-great experience. Latitude, prevailing weather patterns, time of year, and the presence of other hunters can all affect the decision. The ideal campsite often depends on the desired outcome.

Staying Cool, Staying Warm

As most bowhunting for elk occurs early in the fall (often September), what makes for an ideal campsite in bow season may be quite different from what you'd want six weeks later during rifle season. Even at 9,000 feet above sea level, it can get mighty hot as summer struggles to hold off autumn. So locating camp on a north-facing slope in abundant shade makes for comfortable living at this time of year.

You may also face rain or rapidly melting snow squalls. If these are possible in your area, pay attention to drainage at the site. Pitching a tent in a low spot that serves as a catch basin for runoff makes for certain misery if it turns wet. On the first backpacking trip of my life, my two brothers and I made just such a mistake. A torrential downpour started the first night. By daylight a tiny rivulet of water was seeping into the uphill side of our tent and running out the lower, finding its only impediment at the foot of my sleeping bag.

Later in the season, when staying warm is more of a challenge than keeping cool, other factors become paramount in choosing a good campsite. If possible, try to find a location that is exposed to direct sunlight early in the morning. The temperature is typically coldest from just before to just after dawn. Early sunshine helps warm the tent and provides light to the lazy folks who sleep in or have already notched their elk tags. Avoid depressions and creek bottoms, as cold air naturally settles in low spots, a phenomenon that's often noticeable when hiking over uneven terrain. In most cases, flats and benches on mountainsides or ridgelines that finger down from a summit offer the warmest air column in the mountains.

For years, an outfitter camped in a creek bottom below my family's campsite. Perched in a meadow adjacent to an idyllic little

A camp located in south-facing meadow for morning sun exposure.

stream, the outfit's location boasted much that's desirable in an elk camp—grass for horses, a scenic backdrop, and protection from the wind. However, cold air settled into that creek bottom like frost in the dives of a deep freezer. Coupled with minimal exposure to the sun except at midday, the creek bottom was the most frigid acre in the area.

As nighttime temperatures often vary more than ten degrees between elevated locations and depressions in the same area, topographical features are worth noting if you're trying to find the most comfortable place to camp.

Beware the Wind

Wind protection is also important in sheltering a camp from the cold. It seems obvious that a tent located on the brow of an open ridge might be chilled, or even flattened (literally), by a strong blow, but I've seen numerous camps pitched in such exposed places. Erecting your tent on the leeward side of a ridge minimizes wind exposure and the resulting chill. Setting up camp in or near timber offers further protection.

A camp located at the edge of timber for wind protection.

However, take a good look at the condition of the trees near your camp if you pitch your tent among the pines. A tree crashing through the ridgepole will create even more misery than a biting wind. If you spot any decaying or leaning trees that could be toppled by the wind onto your tent, it's a good idea to remove them (if land-use regulations allow it) before you raise the canvas.

Tall dead trees (on left) are potential hazards. Don't set up or move within the drop radius of a snag.

Neighbors in Elk Country

For most folks, passing a week or ten days in elk camp is about solitude and relaxation as well as hunting. But your solitude will suffer considerably if you wind up in a scenic meadow that's crowded with other camps.

If you'd rather not have close neighbors, consider arriving a day or two in advance of other folks to claim your campsite. That's the tactic my family has used for years to ensure that we can camp at exactly the same spot each fall. Although the Montana elk season

Choosing a secluded location reduces the likelihood of crowding from other camps.

opens on the fourth Sunday of October each year, we customarily head in to pitch camp on Thursday, or sometimes as early as the weekend before.

Another way to reduce the possibility of a group making camp right next to yours is to find a location that doesn't lend itself to multiple camps. Large meadows adjacent to roads are magnets for elk camps. Areas adjacent to trailheads and end-of-the-road parking areas also receive plenty of camping pressure. But a smaller, more isolated clearing is less likely to become populated. There's no law that says another group can't plop its tents fifty yards from your own, but a little attention to the site you choose can reduce that possibility.

On the flip side, courtesy dictates that you respect the space and privacy of others when erecting your own camp. "Out of sight, out of mind" is a nice rule of etiquette for elk camps. If at all possible, try to locate your camp out of the sight of others. Furthermore, common decency would dictate that you not "borrow" tent poles cached by another party at an obviously established campsite. Just last season a group of morally questionable souls removed the poles from our long-standing campsite. After cutting new poles, we found the cached ones lying on the ground at another campsite about a half-mile away. Considering the interests of others along with your own is as important in the backcountry as it is at home.

Vehicle Access

Always take a "what if" perspective with regard to precipitation as it pertains to vehicle access to the area of your campsite. Many folks erroneously apply Newton's gravitational theory to mountain roads, assuming that what goes up must come down.

Not so. The site of my family's elk camp is easy to access in a two-wheel-drive pickup with reasonable clearance when it's dry. If it snows, however, the road back down and out often becomes impassable, as there are a few steep hills to climb along the way. On several occasions, we've puttered happily into camp without dropping the pickups into four-wheel drive. Seven days later, we've plowed through four-foot snowdrifts and clawed up icy inclines with chains spinning on all four tires.

So remember to account for how the variables of temperature, wind, and precipitation might affect access to your camp—and your comfort while occupying it. Make a good choice the first time, and your campsite will soon become a place that's viewed not just as a location to raise tents, but a tiny slice of paradise that seems as much like home as the four walls that provide your shelter in the non-hunting months of the year.

— 3 —

PITCHING A WALL TENT

Pitching a backpacking or family camping tent is generally an easy affair. Spread the light nylon shelter on the ground, insert a few slender aluminum poles into sleeves, and up goes the tent. Tap the pegs into the ground, toss on the rainfly, and the camp is set for occupation.

Unfortunately, erecting a wall tent isn't quite so simple. First there's the weight factor. Even a medium-sized canvas tent can weigh around seventy pounds. To support this weight, along with a fly and any snow that might accumulate, a wall tent requires something much more substantial than a wispy aluminum frame.

Discovering that your tent support is inadequate almost invariably comes at the most inopportune moments.

One fall, my older brother, Leroy, and I were camped in the Bighorn Mountains of Wyoming for the opening of deer and elk season. Though we arrived and pitched our tent the day before the opener, dozens of camps were already in the mountains. Some enterprising local hunters had put up their camps some days ahead of time, but had yet to occupy them. Perhaps they were planning to put in a full day at work, and then drive into a completed camp for a leisurely evening before beginning their hunting season.

For one unlucky individual, Mother Nature had other plans. A day or two before our arrival, an early October storm dumped a heavy covering of snow on the mountains—and on the tents pitched previously.

Near the trailhead we used to access our chosen hunting area, we spied a camp. The centerpiece was a most curious wall tent. The sides stood bravely, holding a burden of crusted snow, but the center of the tent was flat on the ground. A few moments' observation revealed that the ridgepole, a homemade affair fashioned from pipe, had collapsed under the weight of the snow. Some poor fellow was in for a rude surprise when he chugged up the rough road into camp, possibly after dark.

Pitched improperly or with an inadequate framework, a wall tent can easily come crashing down in a snow or windstorm. Erected securely, though, the same tent can weather the worst the elements have to offer.

Thanks to fairly recent innovations in outdoor engineering, hunters have many options for creating or purchasing a frame to support their tent. Numerous manufacturers offer internal frames that can be used to pitch a tent anywhere. Some of these can be transferred from tent to tent, others are created for a single tent of specific dimensions. Also available are "hybrid" tent frames, which consist of a ridgepole fabricated from metal tubing with traditional poles or stakes supporting the sidewalls.

A tent pitched with a wide, wood "A-frame."

Even though they are somewhat expensive and bulky to transport, internal frames can be used almost anywhere and are easy to set up. Working together, two experienced hands can set up a tent in less than thirty minutes—an impossible feat with a pole frame. This is a distinct advantage in times of threatening weather or impending darkness.

Of course, you can also erect a wall tent like the adventurers of bygone decades. Wall tents were originally supported by frames fashioned from poles hewed or sawed from nearby trees, most typically lodge pole pines.

Selecting a frame style involves a number of factors related to price, mobility, weight, and aesthetic sensibilities. Pole frames cut from trees are cheap, costing only time and sweat, but they take some skill to fashion and certainly aren't an option if your wapiti pursuits take you into the foothills or prairie, where straight, dead trees are scarce. Still, a pole frame is typically the most sensible option in the backcountry, where the back of a pack animal could be more productively used to carry food or other essentials rather than an internal tent frame.

No matter what type of tent frame you choose, the best way to avoid frustration in the field is to get familiar with it prior to establishing your camp. Puttering with tent frames and accessories has prompted me to pitch a wall tent in my backyard on more occasions than my wife cares to remember. But the neighbors don't seem to mind, and my three children have passed many blissful nights slumbering in the tent just out the back door, even in the dead of winter. On one occasion, the trial run at home revealed an internal frame whose brackets were set at the wrong angle, necessitating several hours of work to correct the problem—something I'm glad I didn't discover at dusk in the mountains.

Pole Frames

At our family camp in the Snowcrest Mountains of Montana, pole frames still reign supreme, at least for now. This is probably due to the fact that my Uncle Tom, the senior member of the camp, still likes the traditional aura of the pole frame. And we've been pitching our tents in exactly the same spot for a half-century and have poles cut to fit them. The poles are left standing each fall in the timber behind the camp. We don't have to scout for and cut new poles each time we erect the camp, so setup is relatively easy.

There are many variations to constructing a pole frame with existing materials. Although some outfitters or traditionalists may champion one design over another, they all function well as long as the materials are sufficiently strong to bear the weight of the tent.

Cut dead trees only to create your wooden tent poles—but first check land regulations about cutting.

Finding Good Poles

With all types of pole frames, the integrity of the structure depends directly on the quality of the poles. An ideal tent pole isn't excessively heavy, but it should be strong enough to support the tent even with a heavy load of snow or under the stress of high winds. Where available, look for the aptly named lodge pole pines. Long before miners and explorers used them to support canvas tents, the plains Indians recognized the strong, lightweight evergreens as the ideal material to support their lodges or teepees.

Standing dead trees make the best tent poles. Poles lying on the ground are often weakened by rot, even if they don't show any

visible signs of decay. If you use fallen trees
for poles, give them a stress test, such as hop-
ping up and down on them. Forest Service
regulations typically prohibit the cutting of
live trees without a permit, but even if this
was legal, poles cut from live timber have
other disadvantages. For one, green poles are
much heavier, making it harder to raise the
tent. They're also full of pitch, which can

*The basic wide A-frame construc-
tion calls for seven main poles to
support the tent.*

make a sticky mess of the canvas and your hands. And green poles
may flex so much that a tent will sag after a few days if not additionally supported.

Obviously, the thicker the pole, the greater its strength. But a
stout pole is also a heavy pole. As a general rule, try to find poles
with a four-inch butt on the slender end. Smaller, lighter tents can
be pitched with slightly thinner poles. As the ridgepole supports
the most weight, use your best pole here.

Creating a Wide Pole A-Frame

One of the most common pole frame designs utilizes two crossed
poles on the front and rear of the tent to support the ridgepole.

*Lash the leg poles together to form
an X, creating the crotch that holds
up the ridgepole for the frame.*

Two other poles are attached to these to hold
up the sidewalls. This wide A-frame design
requires minimal work to secure the sidewalls, but a certain amount of precision is
necessary in the placement of the crossed
poles (the A-frame).

To construct this frame, select four poles of
roughly equal length that will reach from the
peak of your tent to the ground along the
gable ends, with a couple of feet to spare.

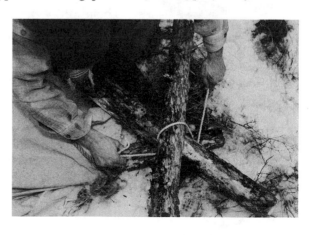

Trim the branches from wooden tent poles to protect the tent from snags and tears.

Lash the eave pole ends to the leg poles of wide A-frame.

Estimate the length for these poles, which serve as "legs," by doubling the height of your wall tent from the peak to the ground. Also, select three poles for the ridge and sidewalls that are about two to three feet longer than the length of your tent.

Using several wraps of stout rope, lash together two of the poles that will support the ridgepole. The lashing should be located roughly eighteen inches below the smaller ends of the poles. The ropes should be tight enough to keep the poles together when crossed, but not so tight that they bind or break when the poles are raised. Their lashed tops form a crotch in which the ridgepole will rest. To fasten these poles together permanently without rope, drive a heavy spike through them, then bend the end over to keep it from working back out. Remember to first bore a pilot hole with a brace and bit or cordless drill to keep the wood from splitting. Repeat the procedure with two other poles.

With the tent spread out in the desired location, insert one of the remaining poles through the openings in the canvas at the peak of the tent. This will serve as the ridgepole. The pole should extend about a foot beyond the canvas at either end of the ridge. Before running this pole through the tent, trim the stubs of any remaining branches that might catch on the canvas.

Place one end of the ridgepole in the top-end crotch formed by two of the poles that you've lashed or spiked together. Secure the ridgepole to the leg poles with a length of rope then raise it until the bottom of the tent is just touching the ground. The leg poles should now extend from the peak of the tent along or slightly above the gables. Check this by extending a corner of the sidewall to the desired height. If the poles don't reach, readjust their height

or the position at which you've secured them together until they do. If they're too long, trim length from the butts of the poles. On frozen ground the leg poles might want to slide. Once they're positioned, drive tent stakes against the bottoms of the poles to keep them in place.

Repeat the procedure on the opposite end of the tent. If you don't have enough manpower to keep the frame from leaning or collapsing while you raise the second A-frame that supports the ridgepole, run a guyline from the top of the crossed poles on the opposite end of the tent to the ground. Then let the frame lean against the line for support.

Tie the tent guylines to the eave pole on the wide A-frame tightly enough to keep the tent from sagging.

The ridgepole should settle securely into the crotch created by the X-shape of the leg poles, and then lash it in.

A variation: a tent pitched with a narrow A-frame and wood sidewall support stakes.

At this point, your tent should be supported on both ends, with the ridge raised to its full height. Once you've determined the ideal length from the butt of the poles to the point at which they cross to support the ridgepole, measure it. Record the measurement so you can use it next time you pitch the tent.

Position one of the two remaining poles on the A-frame legs on one side of the tent. Extend the tent sidewall to determine the proper height for this support pole, and then lash it to the two legs on either end. Ideally, this sidewall support (eave) pole should be lashed on the leg poles equal to or slightly above the height of the sidewall. Tie guylines along the sidewall to this pole, or for a sturdier frame, run them over the pole and stake them to the ground. As you secure the guylines

(Right) A close-up of sidewall support stakes and guylines. Note the forward guyline extending forward of the front of the tent.

(Below) Head-on view of a narrow A-frame tent. Note the guyline extending from the ridgepole joint to the ground in front of the entrance.

Sometimes, you can utilize live trees as ridgepole and eave pole supports, lashing the poles against limbs or trunks.

along the sidewall, check to make sure the bottom of the sidewall stays at ground level or just slightly above. Repeat the procedure on the opposite side of the tent. If the sidewall support poles or the ridgepole seem to sag in the middle, add a center post for extra support, especially if you're pitching a large tent.

At this point, you're ready to stake the tent. It's a good idea to start on the door end. The stakes should be positioned so that the canvas is taut, but if it is too tight, you'll have a hard time opening and closing the door. First stake the door, and then move out to the corners. After you've staked the front of the tent (with the door closed), check to make sure the door opens easily. If it does, stake the remainder of the tent.

For some people, staking the sidewalls of the tent before attaching guylines to the eave poles seems simpler. Which task you perform first doesn't matter, as long as the tent is staked securely to the ground and the guylines on the tops of the sidewalls are tight.

Guylines should now be staked out from the four corners of the tent. Also run a guyline from the peak of the ridge at both ends to the ground and stake it securely to provide extra stability in high wind. I recommend that you attach the guylines to the ridgepole before you raise it.

If you can handle the additional weight, a manufactured wall-tent frame eliminates all the cutting and lashing of poles.

Creating a Narrow Pole A-Frame with Sidewall Support Stakes
Another way to construct a pole A-frame involves a similar support structure for the ridgepole, with wooden stakes propping up the sidewalls. Shorter poles can be used to support the ridge with this method, and fewer long poles are required overall.

To pitch a tent with this narrow A-frame, select four poles that are about four feet longer than the center height of your tent. Then choose a ridgepole that is roughly two to three feet longer than the tent.

Now cut support stakes for the sidewalls. First, count the number of guylines or grommets on each side of the tent. Then, with a tape measure or a stake that will serve as a pattern for the others, mark the distance from the ground to the top of the sidewall. Finally, cut a stake to the measured length for each grommet or guyline on the sidewalls of the tent. These stakes should be strong but don't need to be nearly as heavy as the ridgepole or the poles supporting it. Saplings two to three inches in diameter or thin standing dead lodge pole make excellent sidewall stakes.

To erect the tent, first spike or lash the four support poles together in two pairs, crossing them to form a crotch about a foot below the tops of the poles. Thread the ridgepole through the canvas at the peak of the tent until it protrudes at both ends. Lash the ridgepole to the support poles and add guylines. Raise the ridgepole at the ends of the tent and stake the guylines at both ends.

Next, stake the four corners of the tent to the ground, fully extending the canvas without over-tightening it. Then stake the bottom of the tent along the sidewalls and the ends.

At the front corners (the door end), hold a sidewall support stake perpendicular to the ground with the grommet resting on top. Run guylines out from the top of the stake, one in line with the gable end of the tent and one in line with the sidewall. Stake the guylines and tighten. Check to make sure the door opens freely.

Moving to the rear corners, repeat the procedure for installing and securing the sidewall support stakes. Once the four corners have been staked, use the same technique to secure support stakes at each grommet on the sidewalls. Dry two-by-twos, available at nearly any lumberyard, are inexpensive and make excellent sidewall support stakes, as long as they're free of large knots or other defects. Cut them to length at home and bring them along if you have room; they'll save you from having to locate and cut stakes when you hit your campsite.

Variations

There are a number of other ways to construct pole frames. If there are straight, standing trees adjacent to where you wish to pitch your tent, it's possible to lash one or both ends of the ridgepole to a tree. This is also true for eave poles. Attaching a ridgepole or sidewall support pole to a tree is generally much simpler than supporting one with poles you have to cut, and much sturdier. Don't worry if your pole frame doesn't look exactly like a backcountry outfitter's. If it's strong and keeps the tent standing, it has accomplished its purpose.

Internal Frames

Internal tent frames are a valuable innovation for any elk camp without access to wood poles, and they go up fast. Just last season an internal frame finally made its debut at my family's elk camp. While three other fellows put together a frame of wooden poles for the sleeping tent, I set up the smaller cook tent with an internal frame. Before they'd even raised the ridgepole on their tent, I had mine up and was happily staking the sidewalls.

An internal frame is basically a collection of interlocking pipes that supports a wall tent from the inside. Made from thin-walled aluminum or steel pipe, internal frames are relatively light and surprisingly strong. However, they do come with some disadvantages. Compared to a pole frame that can be adapted on-site to account for uneven ground, internal frames are less forgiving. And they're expensive. A manufactured internal frame can easily add over $400 to the price of a medium-sized wall tent.

One cheaper alternative to a manufactured frame is to buy a set of joints and build the frame yourself. Several companies (like Kwik Kamp) sell joints that accommodate a pipe of specified diameter. The user cuts pipe (typically metal electrical conduit) for each span, and the joints connect the pipe at the corners, eaves, and rafters. Some joint kits adjust for tents of various dimensions and sidewall and ridge heights. For others, the user must supply the manufacturer with the tent's dimensions so that the angle of the joints can be

Parts from a Kwik Kamp joint kit for making an internal frame. Where they go quickly becomes obvious.

The middle joint of a frame kit, forming a connection for roof and side pieces.

matched to the tent. Either way, for a modest investment the handy hunter can create a custom internal frame that functions as well as a manufacturer's frame, and for a fraction of the cost.

Pitching a Tent with an Internal Frame

Whether you use a homemade frame or purchase one from a supplier, the basic procedure for pitching a tent remains the same. First, assemble the entire frame, excluding the legs, where you plan to place the tent. Then drape the tent over the frame. Starting at one corner, raise the tent and frame, then insert a leg in the joint. Repeat the procedure until all the legs are extended upright on one side of the tent. Then raise the opposite side of the tent using the same technique.

Once the tent is raised, straighten any legs that may have moved while you were inserting others. Beginning at the front of the tent with the door closed, stake the corners of the sidewalls at the bottom. Check to make sure the door opens easily, and then stake the back corners and the sidewalls.

Next, drive stakes in the ground for the guylines at the top of the sidewalls. Stake the guylines at the corners first, running two lines for each corner. Place one ground stake in line with the sidewall about three or four feet from the tent, and the other in line with the front or rear panel of the tent. Starting on one side, tie the corner guylines to the ground stakes, supplying enough tension to bring the sidewall perpendicular to the ground, but not so much that it leans toward the stake. Moving to the opposite side, attach and tension the corner guylines in the same manner. Now attach the remaining lines along the sidewalls to ground stakes. Finally, stake guylines from either end of the ridge of the tent. If the wind is blowing while you're erecting an internal frame, stake and lightly tension guylines at the ends of the ridge to help secure the tent. Leave enough range of movement to make necessary adjustments.

Rope Tensioners and Guylines

Rope tensioners (locks) make the job of tightening guylines easier than tying knots. They come with some tents or can be purchased separately as an accessory. A tensioner is a flat rectangular or oval piece of metal or wood with a hole bored through either end.

To use a tensioner, first tie a guyline to a grommet on the sidewall. Then pass the guyline through one hole in the tensioner and back out the other. To keep it from slipping back through the hole, tie a single overhand knot in the rope. Pull on the slack rope between the holes in the tensioner to form a loop in the guyline. Pass this loop over a ground stake and slide the tensioner up the guyline toward the eave of the tent until you achieve the desired tension. The tautness of the rope binds the tensioner on the line, making it easy to tighten the guylines to the ground stakes with one hand.

Without rope tensioners, you'll have to tie knots to secure the guylines to the ground stakes. Many hunters simply take a wrap or two of rope around the ground stake, and then knot the guyline to the stake at ground level.

This procedure works fine in dry weather. But if it snows before you break camp, guyline knots secured to ground stakes may become frozen and nearly impossible to remove without cutting. A better method, which also allows easier adjustment in the tension of the

GUYLINES

If the supplier doesn't include guylines with your tent, you'll need to acquire rope and cut your own to secure the sidewalls and the ridge ends. Quarter-inch rope is ideal, and the type of material doesn't matter as long as it isn't too stretchy. Natural sisal rope works well because it holds knots securely and doesn't stretch, but braided nylon is also fine. Cut guylines twice the height of the sidewalls and secure them to the grommets on the eaves (at the top of the sidewall). So if your tent has five-foot sidewalls, use ten feet of rope for the guylines. Attach two at each corner. Make the guylines that secure the ridge ends two and a half times as long as the distance from the ground to the peak of the tent.

A rope tensioner on a guyline. These operate by harnessing the tension to brace the rope in place.

lines, is to tie a nonslip loop in the guyline about eighteen inches above the ground stake. Pass the guyline around the stake and tie it to the loop with a quick-release knot. This way, the lines are easy to adjust and will come free from the ground stakes even when frozen.

Hybrid Frames

As sidewall stakes are much easier to obtain on-site than a ridgepole and the four additional poles required to support it, a hybrid frame with a manufactured ridgepole and wooden sidewall stakes is a lighter, more portable alternative to an internal frame. Such frames often come from the manufacturer with metal stakes for the sidewalls, but if you're really trying to scrimp on weight, these can be left at home in favor of wooden stakes cut at camp.

Depending on the type of ridgepole, the procedures for erecting the hybrid frame and tent may vary. Some manufactured ridgepoles are supported by an A-frame constructed of metal tubing with two legs on either end. To pitch a tent with this type, proceed as you would with a narrow A-frame of wooden poles. Slide the ridgepole through the tent, and then raise it at either end. Next, stake the bottom of the sidewalls with tent pegs. Finally, place wooden support stakes along the sidewalls with ground stakes and guylines.

Other manufactured ridgepoles are constructed with a single leg extending to the ground. The best technique for pitching a tent with this type is a bit different. First, lay the tent out in the desired location with the door closed. Then stake the four corners with tent pegs. Using a sidewall support stake at each corner, raise the sidewall by running guylines from the top of the stake to the ground in line with the sidewall and the end wall. When you're finished with the first corner, the tension on the guylines on one side and the weight of the tent on the other should hold the stake upright. Repeat this procedure on the other three corners. When you finish staking the corners the tent should look something like an oversized canvas bathtub, with the sidewalls up but the center of the tent still flat.

Open the door and crawl inside the tent. Place the ridgepole in the appropriate position at the peak of the tent and assemble as required. Starting at the rear of the tent, raise the ridgepole by putting the single leg that supports it in place. Repeat at the front. Next, stake the rest of the sidewalls and run guylines from the ridgepole. Staking the four corners before raising the ridgepole allows the weight of the canvas to keep the ridgepole with the single leg at either end in place—a feat that's nearly impossible to accomplish if you try to raise the ridgepole first.

Securing the Fly

With the tent pitched, there's still one chore to complete. If you're going to use a rainfly, which I strongly recommend, now is the time to put it on. First, spread the fly out on the ground next to the tent. Then attach about thirty feet of light rope or parachute cord to grommets toward the ends of the fly. Weight the cords with a stick, stone, or other object, then toss them over the tent. From the opposite side of the tent, you can easily pull the fly over with the attached ropes. When it's positioned correctly over the tent, secure it to the ground stakes that hold the guylines for the sidewalls.

Tent pitched and fly secured—it's time to move in. Coffee anyone?

— 4 —

HEATING

As the wind shifts perceptibly to the north, cold comes creeping down the mountain. Hiking back toward camp at dusk, my breath comes in thick, white puffs and a light breeze stings my cheeks. The temperature hit forty-five degrees at midafternoon, but within a couple hours a cold front has chased it down into the single digits.

It's chilly enough that I'd hate to pass the night in a backpacker's tent, but tonight I'll sleep in comfort. With a wood-burning stove in the wall tent and a stack of dry, newly split pine just outside the door, shivering through a cold night is the last thing on my mind. I'm much more interested in what Uncle Tom is rustling up for dinner.

My sleeping arrangements haven't always been so cozy. I've spent my share of nights in hunting camps with unheated tents, too cold to sleep but hours from daylight, in a chamber of torment that is surely the devil's own invention. Beg, borrow, or steal if you must, but don't create an elk camp without a heating source for your tent. Here are some options to consider.

Wood Stoves

They come in all types and sizes. Some will handle three-foot logs as big around as a man's thigh. Others won't take chunks of wood much longer than a foot or more than several inches wide. Some will last a dozen seasons, others nearly a lifetime. But no matter the style, wood-burning stoves are an amazingly efficient means of heating a wall tent,

A small sheet-metal stove might provide all the surface area you need to heat a smaller-sized tent.

and they evoke an aura of nostalgia that you just don't get from a propane or liquid-fuel heater.

Burning Wood Safely in a Wall Tent

Several years ago, after I'd written an article for a magazine about hunting camps, a caller interrupted my Saturday morning breakfast of oatmeal. He had some questions. One involved my recommendation of wood stoves for heating wall tents. It seemed downright irresponsible and very unsafe, he informed me in no uncertain terms. Why, he'd even called a wood-stove company and asked about it. He was told that their stoves weren't designed for tents and that it didn't sound wise to put one there. What was I trying to do, get people killed?

I answered his question with a few of my own. Had he explained that he wasn't intending to plop the weighty wood-burner in a nylon family camping tent? "No." Did the manufacturer he assailed specialize in stoves for wall tents? "No." Did he know that my family had been heating tents at elk camp with wood stoves for five decades without a single death by flames, asphyxiation, smoke inhalation, or heat stroke? Again, "No"—the proverbial strike three.

Of course, wood stoves *can* be dangerous if improperly used. It's imperative to keep the stovepipe free of obstruction, use a spark arrestor where fire danger outside the tent warrants it, and monitor the dampers to keep the stove from getting too hot. Also, if your tent is constructed of a more airtight fabric than breathable canvas, you must make some provision for fresh air flow from the outside to keep the combustion of wood from consuming all the oxygen in the tent. And always keep flammables away from the stove. Pay attention to these simple precautions, and you're ready to enjoy the warmth and ambiance that only a woodburning stove can provide.

Choosing the Right Stove

You can further increase wood-stove safety by matching the size of your heater to the size of the tent. Other factors being equal, a stove with greater interior volume can burn more fuel and produce more heat. Folks sometimes get into trouble by attempting to heat a large tent with a small stove. In their desire for more heat, they burn the unit too hot, increasing the risk of igniting nearby flammables and reducing the life of the stove. As a general rule, err on the large side. If a big stove is blasting you out of a small tent, just turn down the thermostat—open the tent flap.

Cylinder Stoves' steel stove comes with a flat surface for cooking and radiating heat.

If you're unsure what size stove is right for your tent, purchase one from a dealer that specializes in wood stoves for wall tents. They will usually be able to provide a handy chart that matches their stove models to tent sizes.

Material, weight, and construction are other considerations in purchasing a wood stove. In bygone days, wood stoves that heated homes were typically constructed of cast iron, a material still used by stove builders today. Cast iron can stand years and years of firing without significant deterioration; however, it is often brittle. A sharp blow to the side of a cast-iron stove with a hard object can produce a crack or break. Cast iron is also heavy. But if you don't mind the extra weight and transport it carefully, a cast-iron stove will make a fine tent warmer and may double as a heat source for a garage or workshop at home.

Also weighty, but more durable than cast iron, are stoves built from steel. A number of manufacturers construct such stoves specifically for use with wall tents. In my estimation, these are the finest stoves available to elk hunters, especially those who aren't packing a camp into the backcountry. The doors and dampers on steel stoves aren't likely to warp unless heated excessively, and these stoves can withstand the bangs and bouncing of backcountry travel with ease. If used as intended, a quality steel stove may actually outlive its owner.

While steel is a superb material for wood-burning stoves, not all steel heaters are created equal. Here is a short list of things to consider when evaluating a steel stove:

- How thick is the material? If it's thin, durability is compromised. If it's too thick, the stove will weigh so much you may wish your pickup was equipped with a forklift.
- Does the door open easily and fasten tightly? Poorly fitting doors tend to smoke and some door catches are awkward to operate.
- Does the damper slide or rotate without binding or catching? I've used stoves that required a hammer or rock to tap the damper open and closed.
- Is there a flat surface for cooking or warming? If you plan to cook on your wood stove, use it to warm water for beverages, or keep the stewpot steaming, make sure it has a flat surface on top large enough to accommodate cookware.

Small, sheet-metal stoves are lightweight and ideal for horse packers.

Stoves fashioned from sheet metal are generally cheaper and lighter than steel stoves, but far less durable. The doors on these stoves don't close as tightly as those made of cast iron or steel, and they are usually more finicky to operate. Nonetheless, they have their place in certain camps. Where controlling weight is important, an artfully constructed sheet-metal stove makes a good choice. Some "packer" models even collapse for transportation in the panniers of a pack animal. However, unless you plan to do lots of backcountry camping, you'll probably find a standard sheet-metal stove more suitable.

Barrel stoves made from a kit are another easy, do–it–yourself approach to heating.

Evaluating a sheet-metal stove is similar to assessing a steel one. Check out the doors and damper, and pay attention to the gauge of the metal, which will affect its durability and longevity. If you choose sheet metal, a fussy attitude toward its use and maintenance will greatly prolong its life. Every time you fire it, cover the bottom with an inch or so of dirt or sand to keep it from burning out. Also take great care not to overheat it. Excessive heat weakens the metal and can cause distortion that will warp the door or stove panels. Finally, make sure you store the sheet-metal stove in a dry location because too much moisture will cause rust to form.

Material and quality of construction determine the price of a wood stove. Serviceable sheet-metal stoves generally cost from $100 to $200. For a steel stove, add about another $100. Cast-iron stove prices are quite variable, ranging from around $150 to more than $500. The lower-priced cast-iron stoves are usually of sufficient quality for an elk camp.

Barrel Stove Kits

Perhaps the thriftiest option for an elk-camp stove is the barrel stove, which can be made at home from a kit. A drill, a reciprocating saw with a metal-cutting blade (or a cutting torch), a screwdriver, and a wrench are the only required tools. Treat your barrel stove with the same care you would a sheet-metal stove and it will last many seasons if it's only used at elk camp.

Assembling a barrel stove kit is simple. Just be sure to follow the manufacturer's instructions regarding the procedure. First you'll trace an outline for the door on one end and cut it out with a reciprocating saw or cutting torch. The door is then attached over this hole. Holes are drilled in the barrel to fasten the door with screws or bolts. A similar procedure is used to attach the stovepipe collar to the top of the stove. Finally, legs are fastened to the bottom of the stove with bolts after drilling the necessary holes.

Although most manufacturers advertise that barrel stove kits can be used for fifty-five- or thirty-gallon barrels, a fifty-five-gallon barrel is probably much larger than you need for a tent heater. The smaller thirty-gallon barrel will comfortably heat any reasonably sized wall tent. Make sure the barrel you choose hasn't previously contained any substances that might explode or emit toxic fumes.

The best option is a new barrel, but be forewarned—new barrels typically have an oily coating on the inside that smokes when first fired. They are also usually painted. You'll have to remove the paint before the stove can be used in a tent, as firing will burn the paint and create nasty fumes. When the paint is gone and the kit completed as per the manufacturer's instructions, fire the stove outside a time or two before burning it in your tent. When you can no longer detect smoke or odor from burning paint or oil, the stove is ready for use.

How economical are such stoves? Last fall I put together a barrel heater for less than $50. I picked up the new kit from a discount outlet store for about $40. A friend in the shipping business donated the barrel. Even if you pay

Roof-mounted jacks make it easier to clean the stovepipe. Make sure the pipe extends above the tent's peak.

With a side-exiting stovepipe, some kind of support is needed. Here, a pole secured to a tree does the work.

full retail price for a kit and purchase a barrel it's possible to create a barrel stove for less than $80. Take good care of it and the kit can be transferred to a new barrel when the first wears out.

Stovepipe

As simple as it may seem to connect stovepipe to a stove, there are a few factors to consider before you do so. First, make sure the size of your pipe matches the stove. Don't laugh—I once came within minutes of driving off to an elk camp nearly three hundred miles from home with a mess of five-inch pipe for a six-inch stove.

Beyond the obvious, there are other considerations. Both black and galvanized stovepipe are widely available, but while galvanized is more rust resistant, it also emits fumes and odor when first fired at high temperatures. If available in your area, black pipe is typically a better choice. If you're caught in a situation where you must use galvanized pipe, heat your stove to a good hot burn outdoors with the pipe attached to eliminate fumes inside your tent at a later firing.

Wall tents typically come with a "stove jack" of heat-resistant material, which essentially amounts to a hole in the tent for the pipe to pass through. These jacks are either sewn into the roof of the tent or on a side or end wall.

Want to spark an argument among hardcore elk campers? Ask a group which is better, a stove jack on the roof or one in the side of the tent. Actually, each has its advantages and disadvantages. Roof-mounted jacks allow the pipe to run straight up from the stove without any bends. As a result, the stovepipe draws air efficiently through the stove no matter the wind direction, and it's fairly simple to remove and clean if needed. However, if your tent has a rainfly, it also must have some kind of opening to accommodate the stovepipe. Unless the fly has a moisture-sealing roof jack of its own,

A pipe damper can be a big help in regulating airflow through your stove on really windy days.

To keep hot embers from landing on your tent roof, use a hood-type spark arrestor on the end of stovepipe.

A box-type spark arrestor with a removable screen, much like a furnace filter.

rain or snowmelt can seep under the fly around the stovepipe. And if you try to simply keep the fly away from the stovepipe it might end up covering only a portion of the tent.

With wall-mounted jacks, there is no need for a hole in the fly overhead, so the possibility of a leak around the stove jack is eliminated. Once it exits the tent, however, the pipe must run a considerable distance from the tent or turn and run straight up. Either way, some kind of external support must keep it in place. Additionally, these wall-exiting systems usually don't draw air as well as pipes that run straight up from the stove, and they're often more difficult to clean.

No matter where the stovepipe exits the tent, it should be at least as high as the peak of the tent.

Over the years, we've used both roof-mounted and wall-mounted stove jacks at our family camp. All things considered, I definitely prefer roof-mounted systems.

Two stovepipe accessories are worth acquiring as well: a pipe damper and a spark arrestor.

But if there's already a damper on the stove, why put one in the pipe? Quite simply, a stovepipe damper (or one in the collar of the stove that holds the pipe) better regulates airflow in the stove when a brisk wind kicks up outside the tent. Dampers on the stove and in the pipe make it possible to keep airflow low enough to prevent the stove from overheating when wind outside is "pulling" air through the stove. A pipe damper also helps bank the stove for the night. Reducing airflow with the stove and pipe dampers facilitates a very slow burn, keeping overnight wood consumption to a minimum.

Depending on your stove and the weather, though, completely closing a pipe damper can back emissions up in the stove, causing it to smoke. A similar condition may occur if the pipe damper is

closed when the stove is burning hot. When this happens simply crack the pipe damper until the stove quits smoking. When the stove is burning hot, close the stove damper first, then shut the pipe damper down a few minutes later to avoid smoking.

While a pipe damper regulates airflow through the stove, a spark arrestor restricts sparks or burning embers from escaping through the pipe. Hot embers can damage the tent roof or rainfly and in dry conditions can also ignite a forest fire. Two types of spark arrestors are widely available. One sits on top of the stovepipe and includes some type of mesh material and a hood. The other is usually box shaped and fits between sections of stovepipe near the stove. A metal mesh screen is inserted in the unit much like a furnace filter to keep embers from escaping up the pipe.

Wood warms you twice: when you chop it, and when you burn it.

If you've got firewood lying around at home and can handle the extra weight, bring it — having extra fuel is a safeguard.

Spark arrestors that attach to the top of the stovepipe are generally cheaper, but I much prefer the other type. When burning resinous fuels such as pine and fir, creosote and ash build up fairly quickly on the mesh of the spark arrestor. Cleaning an arrestor that's placed in the pipe near the stove is a simple job—just remove the metal screen, shake it out, and replace it. If your stovepipe exits the tent through the roof, though, cleaning an arrestor at the top of the pipe means breaking down the stovepipe to get at the arrestor and then reassembling it. Also, units attached to the end of the stovepipe tend to foul more quickly because smoke cools as it rises in the pipe and the creosote traveling up to the roof isn't as hot so it collects more readily.

Choosing Good Firewood

"Whatcha cuttin' that gopher wood for?"

Puzzled, my older brother turned from his sawing to face Steve, a Michigan native who had come to Montana for his first elk hunt.

"Gopher wood?" Leroy shot back. "What are you talking about?"

In the hardwood forests of the upper Midwest, Steve explained, no one fooled around with the pine Leroy was cutting for firewood. They called it gopher wood—stoke the stove and then "go fer" more. A nice stack of long-burning oak, maple, or other hardwood was what Steve had in mind for heating the tent, but there wasn't a stick or stump of it within five hundred miles of the elk camp—unless he was willing to take a chainsaw to a shade tree in someone's front yard in downtown Twin Bridges and spend his vacation time in the Madison County jail.

Heat from a wood stove requires fuel, and not just any wood will do. Firing a stove with good fuel is a joy, while fighting with bad wood is a real pain.

In many elk camps, cutting pine, fir, or spruce is simply a matter of walking a few steps into the woods and locating a dry standing tree. In the western mountain states, land-use regulations usually allow for the felling of dead timber for camp firewood, but be sure to check first if you plan to cut on public land.

Although some folks are fussy about the species of evergreen they drop for the fire, any dry standing tree will produce satisfactory results. The cut blocks of larger trunks must be split with an axe or maul, but hefty chunks of split wood keep a tent cozy all night because they burn more slowly than thinner logs. Small-diameter trees are easier to handle, but don't produce as much firewood. Either way, the ideal firewood tree is tall and bare of branches except near the top. "Limby" trees have protruding branches that must be trimmed and knots that make for tough splitting if required. Fallen trees, especially those resting on other trunks or not in direct contact with the ground, can also be used for firewood, but only if they're sound and dry. If the wood appears punky or even slightly damp when cut, use the tree as a last resort only.

Although I generally count on cutting firewood at or near my campsite, if there's any question about availability I throw at least a couple nights' wood in the pickup before I leave home. It doesn't take up much space if packed tightly, and it guarantees plenty of time to find additional firewood after making camp. For trips of just a few days, I sometimes bring the entire supply of firewood to camp.

Laying up a supply of elk camp firewood at home is a simple task. I have a woodpile in the backyard that's used just for hunting camps and the occasional backyard cookout. When I need to trim my own trees, I section the larger limbs for firewood. If I need more, I sometimes acquire lengths of wood from commercial tree-service operations that may be trimming or felling in my neighborhood. Not only does this give me a ready supply of wood each fall, it also allows me to be selective in the type of wood I stockpile. My current stash consists primarily of ash, maple, and black walnut— three hardwood species that burn hot and long, ideal logs for stoking a nighttime stove. I also keep scraps of construction lumber like two-by-fours, which I split for kindling. The kindling and wood are transported in large plastic storage bins that keep things tidy until I hit camp.

Propane and Liquid-Fuel Heaters

Propane heaters are available in many styles, offering an easy heating source for locations where a wood stove is impractical. Although convenient, propane has two main drawbacks for elk camps: safety and cost.

Each year, improper use of portable propane heaters causes the deaths of several dozen people in the United States. Radiant heaters, the type most commonly used by campers, quickly consume available oxygen when used in an enclosed area. If there isn't an opening in the tent of sufficient size to allow enough fresh, oxygenated air to circulate from the outside, the heater can reduce oxygen to a lethal level. Two precautions are imperative for the safe use of propane heaters in a wall tent. First, determine the manufacturer's specifications for outside air flow for your heater. The heater's operating instructions usually indicate what size opening (in square inches) is necessary to provide enough fresh air for safe use. Second, don't burn propane heaters while you're asleep.

Instead, provide everyone in camp with a good sleeping bag. If you must operate the heater at night to warm up, climb out of bed, light the heater, and stand up to stay awake until the tent warms. Then shut off the heater before crawling back in your sleeping bag. If you lie back on your sleeping bag before shutting off the heater and fall asleep, it may consume too much oxygen from the tent and you might not wake up at all.

Another disadvantage of propane is cost. Propane is much more expensive than wood and it can take a surprising amount to keep a tent warm in frigid conditions, even when supplied by a bulk tank. As such, propane is best suited for daytime heating of small tents on short camping trips.

Portable heaters fueled by kerosene or other liquid fuels are sometimes used in elk camps. These heaters generally operate by filling a reservoir. The fuel is then drawn to the combustion unit via a wick or other means. These heaters have similar applications to propane heaters, but they are sometimes quite odorous. Although they're often inexpensive to operate, the same safety issues that plague propane heaters in tents apply to liquid-fuel heaters.

So what's the best way to heat a wall tent—and yourself in the process? As the old saying goes, "He who cuts his own firewood is twice warmed."

For quick food- or water-heating chores, a radiant propane heater, connected to a gas cylinder, is a convenient choice.

5

THE COMFORTS OF HOME

When my dad and his two brothers put together an elk camp in the early 1950s, creature comforts ranked low on the list of priorities. Food, a reasonably warm place to sleep, and elk for the stalking were sufficient for a good hunt.

In those first years, the hunters slept in bedrolls made from blankets on a canvas tarp thrown over a "mattress" of straw. Then someone acquired a sleeping bag. Dad bought an inflatable air mattress. Cots and sleeping pads followed. By the time I was allowed in camp as a teenager, in the late 1970s, a friendly, but semi-serious competition was underway to determine who could configure the most comfortable sleeping arrangement.

Over in the cook tent, a small gas range replaced the primitive, two-burner "camp stove" from the early days. In the oven, Dad and Uncle Tom roasted turkey and ham and created other mouthwatering dishes. Big breakfasts—bacon, eggs, and biscuits—came sizzling from the four burners. In short, unless we put in plenty of miles hiking, elk camp became the family doctor's worst nightmare, an easy place to put on an extra ten pounds and send your cholesterol off the charts.

Cooking and saddling horses in lantern light eventually seemed like too much bother, so one year Tom pulled a generator, a roll of wire, and a dozen or so light sockets from the back of his pickup. After stringing the unsightly mess from tent to tent and out to the hitching rails, he pulled the rope and lit up camp like downtown Bozeman.

Each year, some new innovation seems to make its way to camp. Given the ingenuity of gear manufacturers and the American sporting public's enthusiasm for consumption, there's virtually no limit to the amount of "good stuff" that can clutter an elk camp.

While I enjoy comfort as much as the next fellow, I often question the extent of our investment in time, energy, and finances to create such a luxurious camp. Last season, we had a small camp with just five hunters. Nobody wanted to mess with the generator and stringing up wire, so the equipment stayed at home. I didn't miss it a bit, much preferring the soft hiss of propane lanterns to the clatter of the generator.

Shouldn't elk hunting be something that reconnects us to our roots and reminds us that we can exist happily with less? At the family camp, at least, that philosophy hasn't taken hold. I can't help but ponder the effects of too much comfort-seeking on hunting. Putting together a comfy camp and creating gourmet meals takes time—hours that might be more fruitfully turned to scouting and hunting.

Nonetheless, if you're there for a week or more, the full elk-camp experience can be extremely pleasant. Here are some items that bring the comforts of home to the mountains.

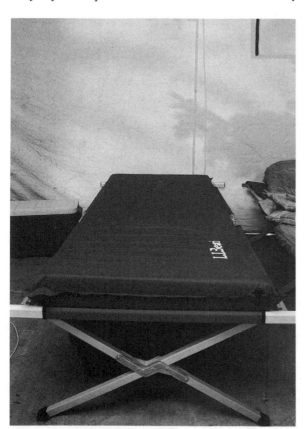

Military-style cots set up and break down quickly, and are relatively easy to transport.

Cots

In some ways, sleeping cots are as much about warmth as comfort. A cot adds thermal efficiency to your sleeping bag by getting your body off the cold ground. The elevated platform also allows boots, backpacks, and other items to be stored out of the way underneath.

I think those army-style jobs are the Cadillacs of cots. They include a wood or metal—typically aluminum—frame and heavy canvas or a similar material, and they fold down compactly for transportation and are surprisingly comfortable. When assembled, three pairs of crossed legs allow some flexibility on slightly uneven ground.

Companies like Coleman and Cabela's have added a number of innovations to the basic army cot, such as a hefty 600-pound capacity, which seems more appropriate for rotund folks in the *Guinness Book of World Records* than elk hunters. More practical features include integrated air mattresses, super-insulating sleeping pads designed specifically for cots, storage pouches that hang from the sides, and coat racks that attach to the end.

There are other sleeping options, but I believe they have some drawbacks. Cots with folding, one-piece legs in the shape of a shallow U are generally cheaper than the army cot. They're comfortable enough too, but they don't fold down as compactly for storage and transportation. On uneven ground the legs occasionally buckle, and these cots are generally less stable.

I've also seen folding beds with air mattresses in elk camp. But the fellow luxuriating on the cushion of air in the evening is sometimes contorted on a deflated mattress in the morning. Leaks are the obvious downside of air beds and mattresses, and even with the notable improvements made in air-bed technology since my dad brought home his blow-up, vinyl mattress, I still believe they're an item more suitable for kids' sleepovers than an elk camp.

> ## LEVELING A COT
>
> A level cot is more comfortable than one listing to the side or sloped from end to end. To do the job right, cut sections of wood of various thicknesses from a dry log. Place the blocks under the legs as needed to achieve a level sleeping surface. Even if your cot is already level, you can add blocks to elevate it a few extra inches to accommodate duffle bags or storage containers that won't quite fit underneath.

The military-stlye cot (left) is better than those with U-shaped legs (right) because its design makes it more stable.

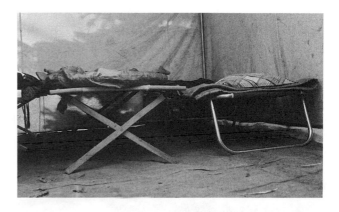

Sleeping Pads

Although a cot raises the sleeper off the cold ground, you'll have a cozier night's sleep with a layer of insulation between your bag and the cooler air that settles near the tent floor. A sleeping pad on the cot is just the ticket, and it can add a surprising degree of comfort as well. The insulation provided by a pad is even more essential when you must sleep directly on the ground.

The advantage of foam sleeping pads is how light they are, and they should last several seasons if kept dry.

There are many types of sleeping pads. For years, my older brother rolled up an old mattress from a single bed and carted it off to camp for his cot. Two- to four-inch-thick open-cell foam, usually available at fabric stores, also makes a serviceable sleeping pad. Roll it up, tie it with cord, and you're ready to go. Foam pads are relatively cheap and will last multiple seasons if stored in a dry location out of the sun.

For youngsters like my boys who can crash on a bed of gravel and pine cones then pop out of bed thoroughly refreshed at dawn, the lightweight, inexpensive, closed-cell pads sold for backpackers provide plenty of cushion and insulation. Aging and honored camp members like myself, though, deserve better.

A few seasons back, I discovered the absolute luxury of a thick, self-inflating pad. Backpackers have long used thin, self-inflating pads that are very light and comfortable. At some point, a crafty engineer decided to design such a pad that was three inches thick instead of three-quarters of an inch. The result was a super-insulating cushion that can be adjusted from spongy to firm by varying the amount of air inside. Unlike air beds, self-inflating pads are much less prone to leaks and don't require a pump. A quality pad isn't cheap—expect to spend about $100—but the support and insulation

are worth the investment for anyone whose
body doesn't adapt well to primitive sleeping
conditions.

Sleeping Bags

*Thick, self-inflating sleeping pads
offer an extra measure of comfort
over a foam pad.*

When I first started using sleeping bags, they
all looked pretty much the same—a rectangular bag with a woven
cotton shell and flannel lining. The thickness of the insulation
varied, but a sleeping bag was a sleeping bag back then. Today,
things have changed. I just finished perusing a popular sporting
goods catalog that devoted a full eight pages to sleeping bags.

What makes a good bag for elk camp? One you already own.
That said, here are a few things to consider.

In most camps, excluding those pitched in the backcountry, a
couple of extra pounds and a little more bulk devoted to a sleeping
bag are insignificant. If you prefer a roomier, rectangular bag to a
tapered or mummy bag, as I do, by all means indulge yourself.
Beyond style, though, a sleeping bag for elk camp must be able to
handle a wide range of temperatures.

I've witnessed temperature variations from minus fifteen to sixty-
five degrees Fahrenheit at exactly the same elk camp in the fourth
week of October. And due to the idiocy, or more kindly, the *incon-
sistency,* of certain people who stoke the wood stove and operate its
dampers, temperatures in the tent can fluctuate from, "Are we in a
sauna?" to "Is there really a stove in here, because I think I'd be as
warm sleeping outside on the ground." Never one to sleep well in
the cold, I quickly learned to pack a sleeping bag that could keep me
comfortable on occasions when the stove went out due to operator
error.

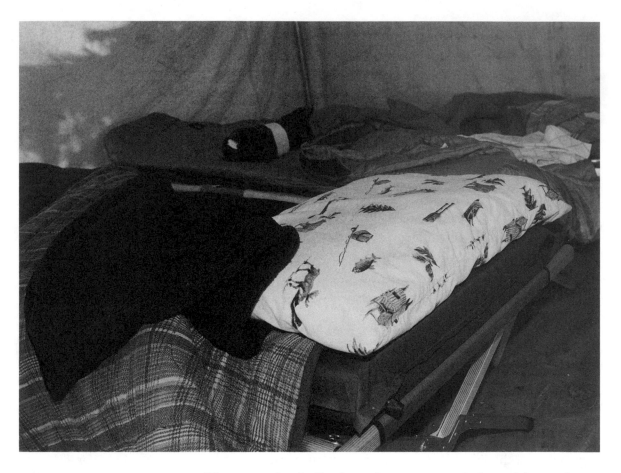

A sleeping bag with a fleece liner works for most people in seasonal weather. Extra blankets help when the snow flies.

However, the bulky bag that conquered the cold wasn't too comfortable when the tent was warm, and I seemed to spend too many hours lying on top of it. Thanks to those seemingly endless catalog pages of sleeping bags, I've found a better solution to a single bag rated for low temperatures. The last time I needed a new bag, I purchased a rectangular one rated for moderate conditions and a Coleman fleece liner that extends the temperature range of the bag down an extra ten degrees or so. When it's warm in the tent, I can sleep in the liner with the bag unzipped. If it gets cold later on, I zip up the bag and pass the rest of the night in comfort.

SLEEPING BAG TEMPERATURE RATINGS

Most sleeping bags are advertised with a temperature rating that is supposed to represent the minimum temperature at which the bag will keep you comfortable. But due to the subjective nature of cold tolerance related to humidity, individual metabolism, and body insulation, a bag's real ability to keep you warm at a given temperature may be much different than the manufacturer's rating.

For example, I'm a thin fellow whose heart seems to have a hard time pumping enough warm blood to feet and hands. From October to April I seem to be cold most of the time, no matter what the weather conditions. So when assessing a sleeping bag I add fifteen degrees to its rating. Thus, a bag the manufacturer rates for twenty degrees really keeps me comfortable at thirty-five degrees. Approximating your own cold tolerance in relation to advertised temperature ratings will leave you more satisfied with your purchase. Experience with various sleeping bags gives the best idea of your own cold tolerance as compared to the manufacturer's ratings. As a general rule, smaller, lean individuals are apt to be at least a little cold at an advertised rating. Folks of above-average size or carrying extra weight (of course, I've *never* seen such a person in elk camp) can probably sleep comfortably in a bag somewhat below the advertised temperature rating.

Clothes Storage

I'm always amazed that clothes packed into a backpack or duffel bag can, once opened, multiply until they take over an entire tent. For some strange reason, elk hunters who may forget their tag or even their rifle at home always seem to take the Boy Scout motto "Be prepared" to extraordinary lengths when it comes to apparel. The average hunter drags along enough clothing to outfit himself for at least twice as long as the anticipated stay in the mountains. In most cases, the weary fellow returns home with as many clean clothes as dirty.

While spouses are generally helpful in making camp preparations, it's best to pack your clothing without consultation. Years ago, the husband of one of my first cousins joined us at elk camp. Thinking herself wise and helpful, my cousin, who shall remain nameless, packed her husband's clothes for the hunt. When he opened his duffel at camp, a change of underwear and clean socks—one for each day in camp—greeted his eyes. I still recall him stuffing clothes into his duffel bag as we broke camp while wondering out loud how he would disguise the fact that of seven pairs of clean briefs he'd worn only two.

The moral of the story is, obviously, to be prepared for the occasion without overdoing it. With a little foresight, it's possible to efficiently store clothing at camp without cramming your whole wardrobe back into the duffel each time you use it.

Cot "trees" are useful for hanging jackets, caps, and other items. A cot tree is a frame of metal tubing that attaches to the end of a cot. Uprights on the frame are equipped with hooks, so the device functions much like an old-time coat rack. A number of manufacturers produce cot trees, but it's possible to fashion one of your own from wood or metal tubing.

When an internal frame supports the tent, you can tie a length of light cord (braided nylon works well) to the joint where the wall of the tent meets the roof at one corner. Then string the cord through the other joints along one side of the tent, or all the way around on three sides. Pull the cord up tight and you have a handy place to hang clothes and other items for storage and drying. Of course, if the sidewalls of your tent get wet, anything on the "clothesline" that contacts the canvas will get damp as well.

Another useful clothing accessory is a drying rack. In my family's camp, the same makeshift rack improvised from slender poles has handled the drying chores for well over a decade. The ends of two upright poles are sharpened so that the rack can be driven in the ground, and two crosspieces are nailed to the uprights. Each fall it

stands behind the wood stove in the sleeping tent—close enough to quickly dry wet outer garments, yet far enough to keep the clothes and rack from burning.

It's also possible to dry clothing on wire hooks suspended over the ridgepole of the tent. As in any dwelling, the air near the peak of a wall tent is considerably warmer than air near the floor, making this area more efficient for clothes drying.

Clothes on a line strung through an internal tent frame.

Gear Storage

Along with clothing, you'll have plenty of other gear to stow in the tent. Rifles, cleaning kits, boots, books, and, as they say in the world of farm auction sales, "items too numerous to mention" all find their way to elk camp. When my uncle Jack was one of the chief ramrods at camp, he constantly harped at people about dragging too much personal gear along. These days, everyone brings as much as they like and we still seem to find a place to stow it.

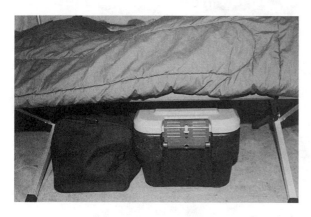

Maximize space by storing gear under the cots. You don't want to trip and fall first thing in the morning.

For the most part, personal gear is stored under the sleeping cots. If you plan ahead by measuring your gear storage containers and duffel bags against the height of your cot, you'll find plenty of room to slide things out of the way. Molded plastic storage boxes with tight lids are great for organizing personal items. They're easy to access, transport compactly and safely, and repel mice.

When pushed for space, one of the best ways to reduce the amount of gear is to avoid duplication. For example, I'll bet nearly every hunter in an elk camp brings his own rifle cleaning kit and alarm clock. Chances are, most of the clocks will return home without waking a single sleeper, and the cleaning kits won't get used unless someone accidentally fills a rifle bore with dirt. There's no reason to carry identical items, be it gun-care products, cookware, or tools (last season we wound up with four axes in camp because we didn't check to see who was bringing what ahead of time).

The one exception to this rule is toilet paper. Seventeen extra rolls won't be much of an inconvenience, but if you forget it altogether you'll quickly find that gun-cleaning patches make a poor substitute.

Hot Showers

In comparison to other cultures, Americans are downright neurotic about bodily cleanliness. People in many other nations bathe once a week, or even less. Most U.S. citizens would be embarrassed to admit they shower less than once a day.

Elk camp is a different story. Grown men who hold important societal positions as bankers, writers, dentists, and engineers crowd into a canvas tent. They exert themselves during the day, working up a sweat. A week later they return home, dirtier and smellier than they've been since last season's hunt, seemingly happier for the filth.

Very early in my camp experience I realized that I'd like to clean up at least once during the week. My first attempt occurred when my cousin's husband, Bill, and I drove two miles down the road to a creek from which we took our water. We were filling empty water jugs at a culvert when Bill decided that a guy could stick his head under the discharge, which dropped a couple of feet into a small pool.

He rummaged in the pickup for a towel and shampoo. Older than me and a smooth talker, Bill somehow convinced me to go first. I splashed some cold creek water on my hair, and then lathered up, thinking how nice it would be to sleep without greasy hair plastered to my forehead. When I stuck my head under the water rushing from the culvert to rinse off, I nearly fainted. The cold was overwhelming—an ice-cream brain-freeze fifty times over.

"How was it?" Bill asked.

"Not bad," I lied.

I took my punishment silently, but Bill yelled like a sissy when the water engulfed his pate. How he drove back to camp with no blood flowing to his brain I don't know. But I guess a guy who decides to wash his hair in an ice-rimmed mountain stream probably doesn't have too much blood circulating in his feeble brain to

begin with. The next year we talked at length about how nice it was to wash our hair, but when we went for water the towel and shampoo were conveniently forgotten in camp.

Nowadays, if the weather isn't unbearably cold, I treat myself to a hot shower instead of culvert water. A few years ago Coleman sent me a water-heating unit to test, complete with a shower attachment. Utilizing a super-efficient heat exchanger, the "Hot Water on Demand" gadget warms water to nearly 150 degrees in ten seconds with a rechargeable battery and a disposable propane bottle. Simply submerge the small pump unit in water and turn it on. As fast as you can ask, "How is it?" hot water bubbles from the spigot or squirts from the shower hose.

When I first brought the hot-water unit to camp, most of my campmates snickered rudely. After I'd rigged an enclosure of sorts over an old stump and spruced up before dinner with just three gallons of water, the ribbing subsided a little. By the end of the week, everyone in camp except one crabby old uncle had lined up for at least a warm-water hair wash. As a smiling Bill toweled off after his turn, he said, "Hey Jack—this sure beats the creek, doesn't it?"

Various hot-water contraptions are now available. If you acquire one for elk camp, keep a few things in mind. First, make sure you plan for the extra water consumption. We found that a person could take a full shower on about two to three gallons of water. Washing hair consumed about half that amount.

When you're finished, make sure that the pump (if so equipped), hoses, and heating unit are completely drained of water and stored in a location where they can't freeze, if possible. Frozen water in any component will likely render the unit temporarily unusable and may cause permanent damage.

I've been well pleased with my Coleman "Hot Water on Demand" unit, which retails for around $170. When not at elk camp, it heats

(Opposite page) A shower enclosure is easy to rig using cut poles and a tarp. Try to locate it in a sunny spot for warmth and light.

water for washing grubby hands and making hot cocoa on family camping trips.

In the absence of a fancy water-heating gadget, you can still enjoy a hot shower. Inexpensive sun showers consist of a plastic water bag attached to a flexible hose and shower head. Chances are, the fall sun won't sufficiently heat water in the bag for a warm shower, but it's a simple task to warm water on a stove and pour it in.

You may also want a portable shower stall. Several companies sell them, but I've found that a four-by-eight-foot plastic tarp and a few slender poles make a great three-sided shower stall. There's a handy stump to stand on at our family's camp that keeps one's feet out of the dirt, but at other locations I've used a small, homemade platform of scrap lumber.

Latrines

Latrine building is not the glamour job in elk camp (where is it a glamour job?), but providing some sort of facility is necessary and an effort well spent—especially if there's a blizzard howling and the temperature has dropped to minus-five degrees, and the toilet paper is flying out of your hands like kite string. A number of options are available for the camp latrine, from homemade pit toilets to sophisticated porta-potties that cost as much as a serviceable pair of binoculars.

When you're really roughing it, and the weather permits, there's nothing easier than digging a hole behind a handy log and, well, squatting. However, you must assume that others will one day camp near or in the same location. So at the very minimum, bury your waste and paper well beneath the ground surface with a small shovel to ensure that subsequent campers don't stumble upon it.

That approach works in most places. But more and more ecology-conscious people are taking along plastic baggies: bag up your dung, drop that in another bag, and truck it out for disposal later. Hey, you have to do it for your dog in most neighborhoods. In popular destinations on public land, it's a courtesy.

Taking a step up in comfort from toileting like a coyote calls for constructing a temporary latrine that can be moved as desired. When a friend's wife started hunting, he built a simple, portable toilet for her (which isn't to say that any woman hunter can't rough it as quickly as any man). The contraption is a plywood frame approximately eighteen inches square and about twenty inches high. He fitted a plywood top to the box and cut a hole cut in the center using a jig saw, while leaving the bottom open. Then he attached a toilet seat over the hole. In camp, he digs a hole in the ground, secures the box over the hole, and sets up a privacy enclosure with a couple of six-by-eight-foot poly tarps and line. Voila— a nice private space where you can think.

A number of outdoor retailers, including Cabela's, offer manufactured privacy enclosures with sides and roofs. In addition to enclosures, the hunter can purchase various porta-potties. The simplest of these are essentially a bucket with a removable toilet seat, requiring the user to dispose of waste after each use. Other more expensive units have a small holding tank which allows for multiple uses before disposal. Some of these come with a water reservoir that provides for flushing and operate similarly to the toilets found in many RVs, but on a smaller scale. These toilets work well, emit few odors, and are comfortable for anyone. They usually cost around $120. However, liquids in both the flushing and holding tanks will freeze in cold temperatures. A frozen porta-potty isn't much fun to empty—or sit on.

Another commercial version of the porta-pottie that is unaffected by temperatures is the Phillips Environmental Toilet, which includes a folding stool and collapsible enclosure/shelter. The unit operates with a single-use bag. In the bag is a powder that solidifies liquid waste and eliminates odor. After use, the bag zips shut and can be tossed in the trash.

No matter how you configure the camp latrine, responsible camping means adhering to two basic rules.

1. Leave no trace: Make sure that your camp doesn't leave behind toilet paper or human waste. Bury it deep, or cart it out.
2. Protect water resources: Human waste can carry multiple parasites, including Giardia. Locate your latrine at least 200 yards from groundwater, including lakes and streams. Avoid ravines or other places that drain run-off or rain water into streams or lakes. Even if waste is buried in these places, erosion can easily wash it to the surface and into natural water sources.

Make It Yourself

Elk camp is an ideal place for do-it-yourselfers. Handy items like cutting boards, tables, and gear storage boxes are enjoyable to build, cheaper than comparable manufactured products, and more rugged. What's more, there's something uniquely satisfying about applying the last coat of sealer to a folding table you've built yourself from scrap lumber versus unpacking one from a cardboard box with the credit card bill still to come.

Do-it-yourself projects for elk camp can be big or small. One fall, quite to his children's amazement, my dad tacked together a small outhouse from scrap lumber, pieces of corrugated roofing tin, and some plywood previously used as concrete forms. He even scavenged a used toilet seat from a location he wouldn't reveal and fastened it over the hole. Thirty years later the outhouse is still going strong—and we're talking function here, not odor.

Storage boxes for lanterns and stoves, portable drying racks, shower enclosures, tables, folding wooden chairs, and a host of other unique and useful items can be created with a little tinkering. As the older generation slowly departs from our family camp, some of the homemade items they've left behind have developed an emotional significance that far outweighs their function. For the handyman hunter, there's a legacy to be left in scrap lumber and ingenuity, even if your exploits in the elk woods aren't worth recounting.

6

LIGHTING

From two miles away and nearly a thousand feet above camp, I maintain an evening vigil. I'm sitting at the base of an evergreen at timberline, hoping a bull will wander out from its bedding area on the north slope below to feed on the yellowed alpine grass. The light expires without activity, so I rise to make the hike back to camp. Far below, the tents stand out like tiny beacons in the dark, each lit with twin lanterns that give a soft golden glow to the canvas.

Topping the final rise above Beaver Creek, I again spot the tents, this time from near enough to make out the shadowed outline of someone sipping from a cup inside the cook tent. The prospects of a mug of hot coffee and dinner put an extra spring in my steps. In minutes I'm slipping through the flap to see what's cooking.

In Montana, where I do most of my hunting, the elk season spans five weeks on the daylight-shrinking side of the autumnal equinox. Even with an early bedtime there are still about three hours of darkness to deal with in the evening. Breakfast and preparations for the day's hunt require another couple hours before dawn. All told, five hours per day might easily be spent under artificial light.

As is the case with most other aspects of camping, the modern-day elk hunter has many more options in lighting than the enthusiastic hunters who pitched their wall tents after returning from World War II. Liquid-gas, propane, and battery-powered lanterns are all now available, along with electrical bulb and wire setups powered by generators or 12-volt batteries.

Transport your lanterns in hard-body carrying cases.

All about Lanterns

If you choose to light your tent with lanterns, don't forget that they require some care in packing. The greatest hazards to liquid- and propane-fueled lanterns are torn mantles and broken globes. Battery-powered lanterns, like all electronic devices, can malfunction after receiving a blow. Protect your lanterns by transporting them in the original containers in an upright position. The cardboard boxes that typically house lanterns do eventually wear out though, so then it's time to invest a few extra dollars in a hard-sided—the best choice—or soft-sided carrying bag made specifically for lanterns.

Liquid Gas

One of my first jobs at elk camp as a teenager involved replenishing and pumping the liquid-fueled lanterns that lit the sleeping and cook tents. Each evening before dark the reservoirs of some four to six lanterns were checked and filled with white gas, or "Coleman fuel" as we called it. The lanterns were then repressurized by pumping. Thus prepared, the camp was in light until morning.

A wide array of liquid-fueled lanterns are still available. They come in single- and dual-mantle models, with varying fuel capacities and options like electronic ignition and the ability to burn unleaded gasoline or kerosene as well as white gas.

Maintaining the mantles and pumps and refueling, which involves funneling odorous gas into the lantern's tank and repressurizing, make liquid-gas lanterns the most labor-intensive lighting sources for elk camps. That said, they still have some advantages over other lighting devices.

For one thing, liquid fuel is cheap. A gallon of white gas goes a long way and can be purchased for about the price of a fast-food meal. Those seeking to wring even more economy from liquid-fuel

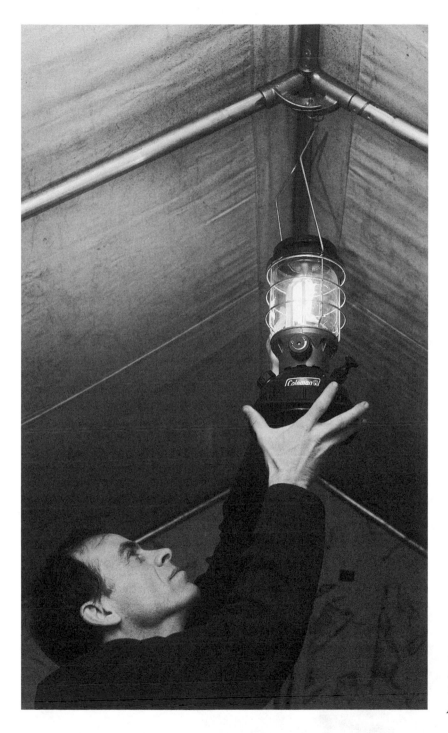

One or two liquid-fuel lanterns should be enough to light a wall tent, when hung from the ridge-pole.

Small lanterns are useful for cooking tasks and gear repairs.

A dual-mantle lantern (left) and single-mantle lantern (right).

lanterns can opt for models that burn unleaded gasoline, which even at today's prices represents a very inexpensive fuel source. And it's available at any gas station—something not true of white gas, batteries, or propane. On the downside, gasoline spills leave a lingering odor that I find much more objectionable than the quickly dissipating smell of white gas.

The most widely available liquid-gas lanterns are equipped with mantles shaped like the stuff sack of a sleeping bag that must be tied to one or two fuel supply tubes. Recently, Coleman introduced a lantern with a tube-shaped mantle that attaches without tying.

For most elk camps, I prefer lanterns with dual or tube mantles because they are considerably brighter than those with a single mantle. Coleman's new tube-type lanterns are exceptionally bright. Last season we tried a lantern with a tube mantle at our family camp and were pleasantly surprised to find that the cook tent, which was previously lit with two dual-mantle lanterns, was adequately illuminated by a single Coleman lantern with a tube mantle.

But both tube- and dual-mantle lanterns consume more fuel than single-mantle models. I think dual- or tube-mantled lanterns are perfect for lighting a tent, while a single mantle is sufficient for outside chores that require less lighting. Compact, "backpack" models like those available in Coleman's Exponent line of products are excellent for backcountry camps. Although these units typically sport just one mantle and have a relatively small fuel capacity, they're bright enough to light a small camp and easy to transport.

Propane

The lighting effect of propane lanterns is virtually identical to that of liquid-fuel lanterns, if not slightly superior. Propane lanterns seem to cast a whiter, cleaner light than liquid-fuel models—without the need to pour fuel into the reservoir and keep the unit pressurized with occasional pumping. To replenish a propane lantern, simply unscrew the old fuel bottle and replace it with a new one. Depending on the model, most propane lanterns will run five to seven hours on a standard 16.4-ounce disposable propane fuel cylinder.

As is the case with liquid-fuel lanterns, propane models are available with single, dual, and tube-type mantles. Again, fuel consumption increases with dual and tube mantles, but they also produce more light.

You can reduce fuel expense and the need to change cylinders by connecting a propane lantern (or lanterns) to a bulk propane cylinder. Sometime in the 1980s, our camp eliminated liquid-fuel lanterns in the cook tent. As we already had a bulk propane tank that ran the cookstove, we easily ran a hose from the tank to two propane lanterns hung from the ridgepole.

Another option for bulk cylinders is a Coleman upright distribution tee, which attaches directly to the cylinder. The thirty-inch tee has an outlet on top for a lantern and two other outlets below for

> ## LANTERN REPAIR KITS
>
> Along with fuel, it's a good idea to take along some replacement parts for propane and liquid-fuel lanterns. For propane, a spare globe and extra mantles will take care of most problems. For liquid-fuel lanterns, a spare globe, mantles, a pump repair kit, and an extra generator will handle nearly any repair. Place the spare globe in a protective container for transportation and tuck the other items inside.

Some newer lanterns operate with a tube-type mantle, but are as efficient as traditional models.

Lantern size all depends on the lighting task: use smaller models for tasks at hand, larger ones for lighting tents and other areas.

more lanterns or other propane appliances such as stoves or heaters. As it's recommended that bulk propane cylinders be kept outside of tents for fire safety, an "outside" lantern can be attached to the top of the distribution tee with inside units fueled via an extension hose. Based on today's propane prices, expect to reap significant savings in fuel costs by using bulk propane rather than disposable cylinders. Bulk cylinders also reduce the amount of trash produced by your camp—an added attraction for ecologically minded hunters.

It's still handy to have a lantern or two in camp not tied to a bulk cylinder. You can still enjoy the economy of bulk propane for these "portable" lanterns by acquiring an adapter and a special tool that allows disposable propane bottles to be filled from a bulk cylinder.

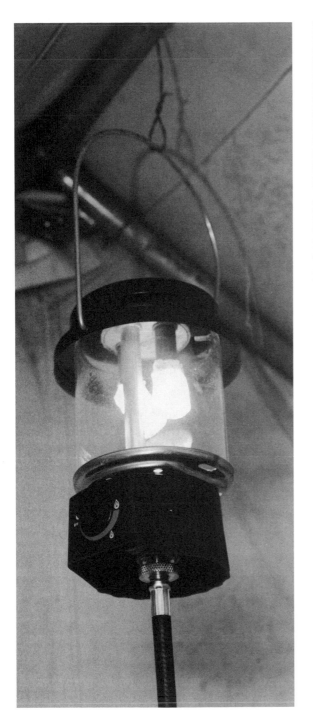

In the back of a tent or where space allows, you can connect a bulk gas cylinder to a hanging lantern for hours of light.

LEAK CHECK

It's essential that propane lanterns and other appliances attach to the fuel source (disposable or bulk cylinders) without leaking. Propane gas is highly flammable, making leaks a potential source of fire or explosion. While leakage isn't usually a problem with disposable cylinders, it can more easily occur with bulk setups utilizing one or more hoses and multiple connections.

Checking for leaks is easy. Simply add a generous amount of dishwashing detergent to a half-cup of water. Brush the solution around the hose and bottle connections. Bubbling in the solution indicates a leak, which usually can be corrected by tightening the connection or replacing a defective rubber O-ring.

Batteries

A battery-powered lantern isn't a lantern in the traditional sense, just an electric light that manufacturers have configured to look like one. Most are lit by one or more fluorescent tubes housed inside the "globe" of the lantern, which is likely constructed of clear plastic rather than glass.

For years I sneered at these lights, wondering why anyone would use a fake lantern. Then my mother gave one to my seven-year-old son as a Christmas gift. As you can't belittle a child's gift from Grandma in public, I told Micah what a wonderful present he'd received and said that it would be perfect for camping. Of course, he remembered my enthusiasm and proudly produced the contraption (complete with remote control) from his bedroom as we were preparing for a winter outing in the wall tent.

As an option, there are battery-powered lanterns with fluorescent tubes.

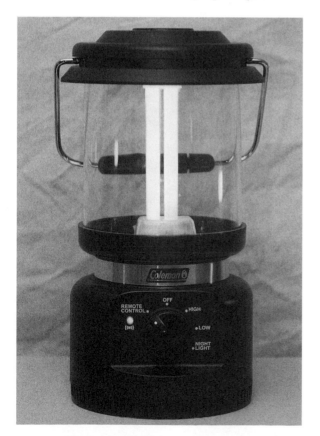

As I found out, battery-powered lanterns are actually quite handy. When one of the kids needed to use the bathroom or get a drink at 2 A.M., I simply pressed the button on the remote. No fumbling for a flashlight or rummaging around for matches to light a "real" lantern. The batteries lasted longer than I expected, and the fluorescent tube emitted a surprising amount of light. And the lantern doesn't produce enough heat to create a fire hazard, so we didn't have to be careful around flammables.

I haven't thrown away my gas and propane lanterns, but I now firmly believe that the battery-powered models have a place in elk camp, especially on shorter outings where convenience outweighs economy.

Most battery-powered lanterns operate on four or eight D-cell batteries, while others utilize a single, rechargeable battery that can be charged from a 110-volt outlet or a 12-volt socket (cigarette lighter). Of course, battery consumption varies in relation to the light output of the unit and the type of batteries and bulb. However, most are quite efficient. Powered with alkaline cells, the majority of models in Coleman's line of lanterns operate for about fifteen hours before draining the batteries. Lanterns with a high/low switch can wring nearly thirty hours of runtime from a set of batteries on "low."

Maintenance is usually as simple as changing batteries. However, the fluorescent tubes or bulbs do burn out after prolonged use, so it's wise to take a spare bulb along as well as an extra set of batteries.

110-Volt Electric Lights

When I was a teenager, the morning alarm in elk camp rattled the sleeping tent at 4:30 A.M. Some older member of the tribe, usually my uncle Jack, chased me from the warmth of my sleeping bag with admonitions to "stoke the stove and get them lanterns lit." By the time I advanced enough in years to delegate early morning chores to the younger generation, a new contraption made the camp-lighting job much easier. All they had to do was to walk behind the cook tent, flip the choke on a gas-powered generator, and give the rope a pull. In an instant the whole camp—tents, hitching rail, and walking areas—was lit up with the same incandescent glow that greets my eyes when I flip the kitchen wall switch at home.

Once wire and lights are strung, lighting a camp with a generator is a breeze. We used a generator and electric lights to illuminate our camp for a decade, although we've since returned to propane lanterns. For one thing, even the best generators can break down. If the thing won't start, you're in the dark unless you've brought along some lanterns for backup. Also, even the new, low-decibel generators create enough mechanical noise to block out the euphonic strains of wind in the evergreens and the far-away yipping of coyotes—sounds of nature I wouldn't want to live without at elk camp.

12-Volt Electric Lights

All manner of recreational vehicles, from popup campers to cavernous motorhomes, are illuminated with lights powered by a 12-volt battery. Wall tents can be similarly lit. Twelve-volt light fixtures are available at nearly any RV center and many auto parts stores. Additionally, most low voltage, under-the-counter lights for interior home use operate on 12-volt current and can be adapted for an elk camp.

The primary advantage of electrical lights and appliances in this voltage is that they present minimal danger of a hazardous shock. Additionally, they can be powered by a deep-cycle battery that is portable. You may already own one for your boat or RV. Unlike lights connected to a generator, 12-volt systems charged by a battery are totally silent, a luxury unmatched even by the low hiss of a propane lantern.

As manufactured, 12-volt light systems aren't available for tents, at least none that I'm aware of, you'll have to design and wire your

A wide variety of 12-volt lights are available for stringing up in camp; some are more practical than others.

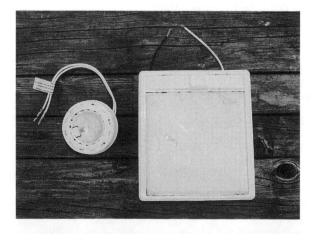

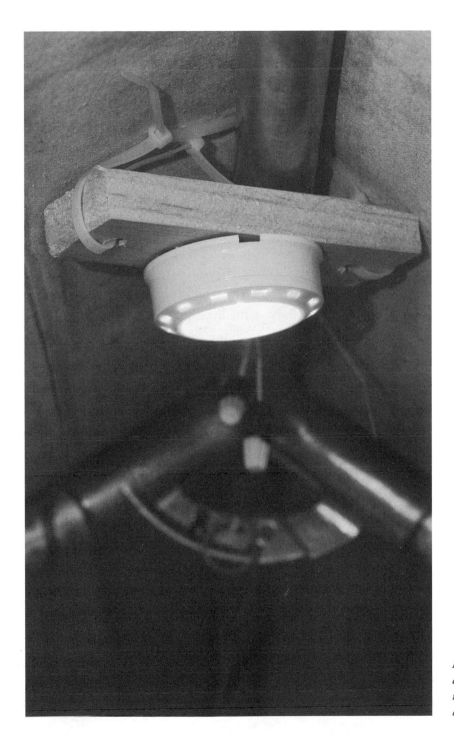

Here's a 12-volt light hung from a ridgepole with a bit of innovative rigging using plastic ties and a piece of wood.

own. While such a project requires only basic knowledge of electrical circuitry, two safety components are especially important. First, even with its low voltage, a short circuit in a 12-volt system has the potential to melt the insulation from wires and possibly start a fire. A simple in-line fuse placed within eighteen inches of the battery will provide the necessary protection. Second, be sure the gauge of the wire you intend to use matches the amperage load of your lights and the length of the wire required to supply them so that the wire can't overheat.

Producing a 12-volt lighting system for a wall tent is quite easy. Start by acquiring the number of light fixtures you need for your tent; two or three interior lights will usually suffice. You might also want to attach an additional outside light fixture on the front of the tent, along one eave at about shoulder level. Use a fixture with a built-in switch so it can be turned off and on independently of the rest of the system.

Next, wire the series of lights so that they can be attached along the ridgepole of the tent. Plastic zip ties work well for holding fixtures to wood or metal ridgepoles. Between the battery and the lights, on the inside of the tent, splice an on/off switch into the wire. After wiring up the lights, attach supply wires to the battery. Gases emitted by deep-cycle batteries are explosive, so to reduce the risk of fire, place the battery in a box outside the tent. To make it easier to move the battery for recharging, attach the wires that power the lights to the battery with alligator clips.

Once the system is installed, a flip of the switch lights the tent. Powered by a heavy-duty deep-cycle battery, a 12-volt lighting system can provide trouble-free lighting for a week's hunt or more, depending on the number of fixtures used and the battery's condition and capacity.

From the timeless simplicity of kerosene lanterns to a 12-volt system complete with halogen bulbs, there are plenty of options for keeping a camp lit after dusk and before dawn. And with new lighting devices popping up every year, I wonder what's next—glow-in-the-dark wall tents?

— 7 —

THE CAMP KITCHEN

If the numerous options in lighting and sleeping arrangements for elk camp seem perplexing, the myriad cooking possibilities can be downright overwhelming. From a wood stove that doubles as a heater to a tiny backpack stove powered by compressed gas whose weight is measured in grams instead of pounds, there are scores of options for boiling the oatmeal.

Stoves, Stoves, Stoves

The cooking stove is central to the camp kitchen, as it often dictates the cookware and menu. Like many aspects of crafting an elk camp, choosing a stove is largely a matter of balancing function and convenience. Larger, more elaborate appliances are the gateway to increased menu options, but they also require more effort to transport and typically consume more fuel.

Somewhere along the line, the patriarchs of our camp forsook their smaller stove for a kitchen-sized gas range. I distinctly remember my astonishment when, as part of the gear-loading chores for my first elk hunt, my older brother and I hefted a huge propane cylinder onto the back of Dad's three-quarter-ton Chevy. Next came the slightly battered gas range, complete with chipped porcelain, four burners, and a creaking door that opened to a substantial oven. It seemed overkill to my aching back, but I kept my mouth shut as the opinions of teenage boys were heeded as often as the grunting of hogs out back in the barnyard.

At dusk, after we'd worked up healthy appetites pitching camp, my

A hearty breakfast is a staple of elk camp.

perception of the stove and its massive propane bottle began to change. Out from the oven came a sizzling ham, tantalizing to the nose and browned to perfection. Buttery mashed spuds, home-canned green beans, and warm apple pie followed. I had no idea that such food could be produced by the cantankerous men I claimed as father and uncles—men who at home played helpless in the kitchen, claiming that the culinary arts were the exclusive provenance of "women folk."

Liquid Fuel

Compact liquid-fuel stoves that operate via a pressurized fuel reservoir are still quite common for backpacking trips, but are becoming increasingly difficult to find in the larger, traditional configurations that were once the standard in nearly every family campsite across the nation. Coleman is one of the few manufacturers that still produces the classic liquid-fueled "camp stove," offering a variety of two- and three-burner models sufficient for all but the biggest cooking chores.

Liquid-fuel stoves and lanterns work much the same way. Most liquid-fuel stoves are designed to burn white gas, but as is the case with lanterns, some will operate on unleaded gasoline. Although propane stoves are easier to operate, liquid-fuel models remain the choice of many backcountry elk hunters who prefer the portability of white gas to disposable propane cylinders. A comparable propane camp stove requires roughly six disposable 16.4-ounce bottles to burn as long and hot as a liquid-fuel stove consuming a single gallon of white gas.

As a gallon of fuel will operate most two-burner liquid-fuel stoves with both burners on high for around five to six hours, a

Small as it is, a backcountry stove fully fueled can turn out a lot of hot food.

Cooking pancakes on a Camp Chef cast-iron griddle, while the eggs fry in a cast-iron skillet on the adjacent grill.

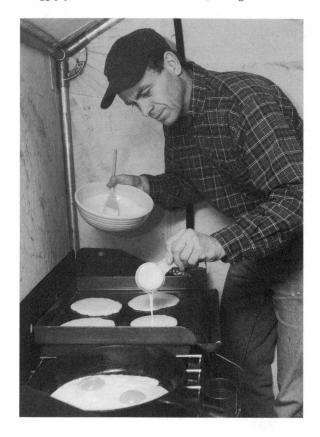

Smaller, propane-powered camp stoves come in handy for making small meals, or for one or two people.

single can of gas goes a long way. And maximum BTUs for two-burner models rival or exceed that of similar propane units. Even the space-efficient, single-burner backpack models provide more than enough heat for routine cooking chores. Both backpack and traditional models boil a quart of water on a single burner in around four minutes.

Propane

We no longer wrestle the kitchen range to camp for cooking, but propane still fires the two cookstoves. At times I miss the ability to bake biscuits or roast meat dishes in a real oven, but I can't say the elk-camp experience has suffered too much without the old range.

As propane rules the world of stove fuel for camping, and propane stoves come in such a wide array of styles and sizes, it's probably more useful to make some general observations about these stoves than to discuss specific models.

For everything but backcountry or spike camps, I strongly recommend a stove with at least two burners. Invariably, while the beef stew is bubbling on one burner, some cold hunter will stomp back into camp looking for a hot beverage. If you're cooking a traditional breakfast, it's nice to crisp the bacon and fry eggs at the same time, yet still have a burner free for brewing coffee. Get the picture?

For casual use, the compact propane "camp stoves" fashioned from sheet metal are perfectly suitable for a small elk camp. For the price of a couple large pizzas, you can buy a two-burner stove at most dis-

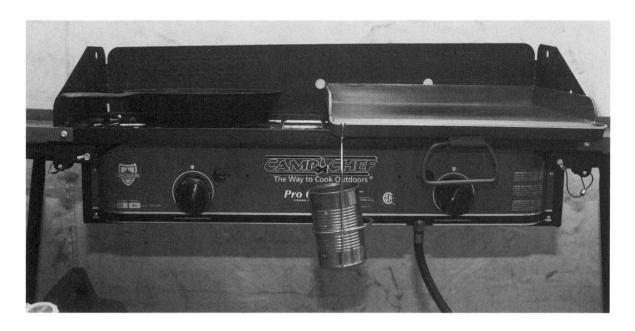

A Camp Chef professional-type stove and cooker is what you need to feed a large party of elk hunters.

count camping stores. However, these budget stoves have two disadvantages. First, due to their lightweight construction, they won't hold up well to abuse and their longevity is limited. Second, their burners don't produce the heat of the larger, heavy-duty cookers. For example, many two-burner, lightweight camp stoves have burners with a maximum heating capacity of 8,000 to 10,000 BTUs. By contrast, most heavy-duty two-burner stoves can generate two to three times that amount.

Available from Camp Chef and other manufacturers, heavy-duty stoves—or cookers, as they're often called—boast more powerful burners than lightweight propane stoves and far greater durability. Standard on these stoves are cast-iron burners, steel grates, state-of-the-art regulating knobs, and rugged housings, which all improve function but also drive the price into the $100 to $300 range.

HEATERS/COOKERS

Some radiant propane heaters also double as cookers. Although these aren't usually as suitable for day-to-day cooking chores as a stove, they work well for warming foods and heating water. When not in use for cooking, they make a great supplemental heating source to a wood stove.

While the wood stove burns, put your coffee pots on a flat metal sheet atop the stove to maximize heat use.

For extended use, especially in a camp that houses more than a handful of hunters, their increased heating capacity and durability are well worth the extra investment. Currently, two Camp Chef cookers of this variety heat our meals—and warm the cooking tent in the process.

No matter what type of propane stove you choose, for anything but the shortest trips you'll want to adapt your stove (or stoves) to a bulk propane bottle. Chances are you already have one. Come elk season, a number of folks I know simply disconnect the bulk cylinder from their gas barbeque grill at home, check the fuel level, and then head to camp. Adapters and hoses that allow you to connect one or more appliances to a bulk cylinder are available at RV centers, many larger hardware stores, and home centers. Additionally, some appliance shops may be able to create custom hose assemblies for specific camp applications.

The pot with all the crazy squiggles is regular, the lighter pot decaf. Can't have the jitters when you're taking aim.

Wood Stoves

If you heat your tent with a wood stove, it can also double as a cookstove, provided that it has a flat surface on top. To some extent, your decision to cook on a wood stove may depend on the weather. For early-season rifle or bowhunts in warm conditions, stoking a wood stove for cooking may raise temperatures in the tent to tropical levels.

At a minimum, though, a wood stove is great for keeping coffee hot at breakfast and warming other food. To actually cook on a

WATER HEATERS FOR WOOD STOVES

Woodburning stoves are also a great way to heat water. At our camp, we keep a large, enameled coffeepot full of water on the wood stove for hot beverages and dish-washing. Some manufactured wood stoves, like those from the Cylinder Stove Company in Utah, are designed to accept a hot-water heater that attaches to the side. Simply open a spigot on a reservoir to get hot water, just like filling a cup from the water cooler at work.

wood stove, you must maintain a specific and consistent temperature, which takes some practice. The addition of fuel or air to the stove doesn't have the same immediate result as turning up the burner on a kitchen range. Thus, it's easy for the frustrated novice to make the stove too cool or too hot for artful cooking.

There are a few simple steps you can take to achieve more consistent heat in your wood stove for cooking. As when cooking on a campfire, start your fire in the stove well before you plan to cook. A bed of coals in the bottom of the stove will help maintain a desired temperature better than several burning logs. Also, add small sticks of wood sparingly once the stove has heated. For most projects, a temperature that is slightly lower than the ideal simply increases cooking time by a few minutes. But there's no going back once you've overheated the stove and burned breakfast.

Other Cooking Appliances

Although it is possible to keep the camp happily in victuals with a stove, two other cooking appliances are worth adding to your camp kitchen. The first is a gas or charcoal barbeque grill. A number of manufacturers produce compact "tabletop" grills, and despite the low price tag they perform very well. For years I've used a small grill at camp that my wife and I bought nearly two decades ago for $20. When I upgraded my camp stove to a heavy-duty Camp Chef cooker a couple of years back, I added the optional grill box that sits right on the stove grate. The box does an excellent job of grilling, and it saves the hassle of packing fuel canisters or an extra propane hose for a self-contained grill.

While some people are attracted to grilling primarily for the enhanced flavor it gives to food, at elk camp I mostly favor a grill for its convenience. Frying steaks or chicken in a skillet on the stove always seems to create an impressive mess of splattered grease that takes far more time to clean up than the meal does to consume. When the cooking is finished, cleanup on a grill is as simple as replacing the lid and letting the unit fire for a few minutes on high to burn away any residual grease or meat juice.

Another handy appliance in the camp kitchen is an oven. While they require more monitoring than your kitchen oven at home, camp ovens that sit on a stove burner or mount in the stovepipe of a wood stove are capable of handling a variety of baking chores, from breakfast biscuits to chocolate chip cookies. Most models include a built-in thermometer that allows the user to monitor the oven temperature at a glance. Even if you don't whip up things from scratch, you can bring numerous ready-to-bake goods for the camp oven.

> ## AVOID A SMOKE OUT
>
> Never attempt to grill things like burgers or steaks inside a tent. The smoke will chase you into the woods faster than a marauding bear. When it's cold, though, storing your grill inside a warm tent or bringing it in a couple of hours prior to use will allow the unit to heat up more quickly once you take it outdoors for cooking.

Cookware

For centuries, cast-iron cookware has bubbled beans and ham, seared steak, and thickened gravy at countless camps of prospectors,

"TV" DINNERS

You can serve great camp meals with less cookware and in-camp labor by preparing in advance. For a number of years, each family at our camp was required to provide a precooked main dish that just required heating. My mother and aunts would kick in other goodies like pies, cobblers, brownies, and cookies for dessert. This routine produced incredibly good meals and made it possible for everyone to hunt late in the day without worry about the evening meal. Whoever returned to camp first simply warmed one of the main dishes in the oven or on the top of the wood stove.

homesteaders, and hunters. Cast-iron pots and pans fed the stalwarts of the Lewis & Clark expedition over two hundred years ago and are still found in the kitchens of many independent folks who live on the fringes of civilization today.

Although the popularity of cast-iron has waned in recent decades due to the development of high-tech cookware boasting lighter weight and nonstick surfaces, there currently is a revival of sorts in cast-iron cooking, especially among outdoor types who appreciate the tradition and functionality of iron cookware. At camp and home, cast-iron pans, skillets, and Dutch ovens have several features that commend themselves to the cook.

A well-seasoned cast-iron skillet keeps foods from sticking, if it isn't overheated, and distributes heat evenly to the cooking surface. And cast-iron cookware is virtually indestructible. At the family ranch near Three Forks, Montana, my mother still cooks with the same cast-iron skillets she used fifty years ago. Nutritionists have also found that food cooked in cast-iron absorbs traces of iron from the cookware, increasing the concentration of this element in the food. Finally, cast-iron cookware is easy to convert to weaponry. I once read a story of a woman who whacked an aggressive bear on the snout with a cast-iron skillet to drive it from her camp.

When weight is an issue, such as for back-country camps ferried with pack animals,

Breakfast is a priority, so you might want to pick someone who's actually a good cook and make that his main chore.

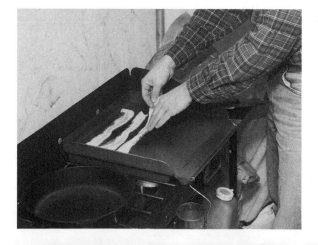

high-tech cookware that weighs ounces rather than pounds is generally the best choice. If you require just the basics—boiling water and frying—it's possible to get by with a single pot and lid; look for a cook set with a lid that doubles as a skillet. Add a small coffeepot and you have everything you need for a minimalist camp.

Lightweight cookware is available at discount stores and specialty mail-order catalogs devoted to camping and backpacking, but beware. Quality varies widely, even among items advertised for backcountry use. The old adage, "You get what you pay for," holds true in shopping for camp cookware. In general, more expensive ware boasts more durable nonstick surfaces, greater resistance to scratches and dents, and superior heat transfer.

If weight and portability aren't an issue, modern cookware from a kitchen or department store is an economical, serviceable alternate to cast-iron or the specialty ware favored by backpackers. Nearly a decade ago I picked up a couple of economical nonstick frying pans for camping that are still going strong, and with reasonable care they should last another decade. Just because a piece of cookware isn't purchased from an outdoor retailer doesn't mean it won't be serviceable at elk camp.

Kitchen Design

Camp kitchens can range from austere arrangements with limited capabilities to expansive creations on which the enterprising chef can turn out anything from flaming

PORTABLE COUNTERTOP

If you or a friend has recently replaced a kitchen countertop or you know someone in the construction business, it's possible to make an excellent cutting/food-preparation board from countertop scrap. Installing a sink in a new countertop generally requires cutting away a two-by-three-foot piece of the top. If you can obtain such a piece, cut it into a rectangle. Then use waterproof glue and nails or screws to attach strips of wood around the perimeter to protect the edges from dings and moisture. A piece from an old countertop can be used for the same purpose.

steaks Diane to sour-cream rhubarb pie. After three decades of observing elk hunters, I've noticed an identifiable trend in camp kitchens. Camps belonging to young hunters, in whom the blood lust still runs high, generally include a utilitarian kitchen. Their daylight hours are spent on the hunt, with little priority given to cultivating culinary arts in camp. By contrast, older folks seem more inclined to value the camping and cooking experience as highly as the hunt itself, and their kitchens reflect this difference in attitude.

No matter how you design your camp kitchen, here are some ideas to consider.

Cooking, food preparation, and cleanup are all easier when you're standing upright at a table rather than hunched over the ground. Small, portable tables are like burners on a camp stove—it never hurts to have an extra one.

THE ALL-IMPORTANT LIST

A checklist of items for the camp kitchen is essential so that nothing is forgotten at home. Besides checking off items on the list when you leave home, take it along to camp. When you think of something you'd like to have along for next year's camp, add it to the list immediately. At the end of the camp, delete unnecessary items as well.

Even when I'm camping solo, I like to have at least two tables. The ones I prefer are about two feet wide by four feet long, with folding legs for easy transport. I place my cooking stove on one table with a metal surface. That leaves enough room on the opposite end for the cooking pots and pans, along with food in use such as canned vegetables, spaghetti, and the like. My other table has a plastic top, which cleans up easily with soap and water. I use it for meat preparation, making sandwiches or salad, and any other chores that require a clean surface. When camping alone or with just another person or two, the plastic-top table doubles as a cleanup area, hosting a dishpan and drainer after the meal.

If you put together a large camp that houses a half-dozen or more hunters, adding a cook tent makes sense. At our family camp

in the Snowcrests, up to a dozen hunters might lodge in wall tents for the first week of elk season. So a separate tent is the only way to go. A rectangular table large enough to accommodate ten hungry adults spans one end of the tent. The rest is devoted to food and water storage and the camp kitchen, which consists of two double-burner Camp Chef cookers and a wood-heating stove with a flat top that also serves as a warming platform for coffee and hot water. Three small tables function as a food preparation area, a stand for the washbasins, and a place for miscellaneous chores.

A well-done breakfast served in a warm, bright tent is the epitome of a comfortable, functional elk camp.

Despite the extra expense in acquiring a cook tent and the additional labor expended in pitching it, the investment is a good one. The cook (or cooks) has plenty of room without encroaching on someone's sleeping spot or bumping elbows with hunters drying clothes or cleaning guns in the sleeping tent. The eating table in the cook tent makes a fine spot for playing cards—or writing a chapter for an elk-camp book—when it's not mealtime. And if a storm keeps the entire crew holed up in camp, the cook tent allows people more room to spread out and pass the time without feeling cramped and confined.

Food Storage

Foodstuffs fall into two basic categories: perishable items that must be refrigerated, frozen, or used in a fairly short timeframe to avoid spoilage and nonperishable items that require no special storage considerations.

HANDY HOMEMADE STORAGE CABINETS

One fall, Uncle Tom arrived in camp with an ingenious storage solution for all of the dishes, cookware, spices, and miscellaneous kitchen items. His creation handles food storage as well. Working with half-inch plywood, Tom made two cabinets with a series of enclosed shelves and a door. He calculated the height, width, and depth of the shelves so that flat plastic storage bins full of kitchen gear slide easily in and out. Handles on the outside of the cabinets make them simple to load and unload from a pickup. Storing everything in the cabinets makes it easy to inventory, organize, and transport cooking gear and kitchen items. A piece of painted plywood spans the cabinets, yielding several feet of handy counter space.

Most perishables except baked goods need to be kept cool or frozen or they'll spoil in a matter of days. As elk seasons typically occur in autumn and elk camps are most commonly pitched at high elevations, the chilly night air helps refrigerate meat, dairy products, eggs, and vegetables. However, in extreme cases, temperatures can fall so low that food stored outside freezes, even in insulated coolers. So the first rule of thumb for the camp cook in storing perishables is to monitor the outside air temperature and the temperature inside food containers.

Perishables that must be kept cool or frozen are usually stored in coolers. If nighttime temperatures drop to around freezing, nearly any type of cooler will work fine. However, if you're on an early season bowhunt or the weather turns unseasonably warm, it's worth

The author's homemade kitchen storage unit.

investing in quality coolers specifically designed for extreme conditions. These coolers are generally more expensive, but they boast
thicker insulation in the walls and lids—some cheap coolers don't
have insulated lids—and a lid gasket that provides a tight seal.

How much better are these high-performance coolers? A couple
of years ago I bought a Coleman Xtreme cooler for summer
camping trips. Packed with comparable amounts of food and ice,
the Xtreme cooler easily doubled the safe storage time of perishables in our standard coolers.

Where you can, stash your coolers in the shadows or shade under trees to prolong the storage of perishables.

No matter what type of coolers you use, a few tricks will help you maximize their efficiency. The first step is to bring the cooler's temperature to the ideal storage temperature. If you can fit the cooler in a large refrigerator or freezer, chill the cooler before packing it. Dragging a cooler from a hot attic storeroom and cramming it with frozen meat, as often happens, allows the meat to thaw while it actually cools the cooler.

Also, large quantities of any material will remain frozen longer than small quantities. For example, a bunch of ice cubes melt much more quickly on a hot driveway than a similarly sized block of ice. So pack food tightly in larger coolers to keep it cold longer.

Organize items in various coolers by intended use to minimize the number of times a cooler must be opened and closed. Breakfast beverages and milk, juice, eggs, and bacon might be kept in one cooler. Soft drinks and other beverages consumed during the day or on a less predictable schedule should be kept in another cooler. Frozen meats will keep longer if packed separately in yet another cooler.

Also, pay attention to where you keep your coolers in camp. A shaded location on the ground shelters coolers from the warming rays of the sun and also prohibits warm air from circulating underneath. Throw a tarp or saddle blankets over your coolers to further aid their efficiency.

Nonperishables are relatively simple to store. Discount and home improvement stores carry a variety of storage bins that make excellent containers for nonperishable food in elk camp.

As with perishables, it's helpful to organize nonperishables by type and intended use to save time spent rummaging through a half-dozen containers to obtain a half-teaspoon of salt. Canned goods can be kept anywhere they're protected from freezing, but other foods may require some attention to thwart those rapacious bandits of the elk-camp kitchen—mice.

I distinctly remember one hunting trip where my older brother, Leroy, and I pitched our tent in a deserted Forest Service campground. After a long day of hunting, we returned to find that our camp had been invaded by legions of mice. Anything that

remotely resembled victuals had been sampled. The little monsters chewed open a box of crackers, nibbled cookies, and chewed into oriental noodle packs, ruining more food than we had to spare. Revenge was in order.

Nonperishable items get stored in a mouse-proof container.

Armed with weapons of mass destruction—two mouse traps and a jar of peanut butter—we plotted a night attack. Within minutes after the lantern died that evening, a distinct *smack* in the corner of the tent signaled the first success in our counterassault. A short time later, the other trap sprang nearby. Sleep was in short supply that night as the sounds of battle frequently jarred us awake. I don't recall the exact number, but well over a dozen renegade rodents fell before daylight.

Had we just packed our food differently, mice couldn't have plundered our pantry in the first place. Nowadays, we make sure all nonperishables that might attract attention are stored in mouse-proof containers. Plastic storage bins with tight-sealing lids fit the bill perfectly. Nonetheless, I never camp in the high country without a couple of mouse traps and a jar of peanut butter—even if they can't get to the food, they can still mess up the kitchen.

And the last thing I want compromised at elk camp is the kitchen. Good meals make for happy campers. As an elderly member of our camp is fond of saying, "The only thing you're taking from this earth is what's in your belly, so it better be good."

− 8 −

WATER

In survivalist circles, the "rule of threes" is often quoted regarding the necessities of human life. Roughly speaking, a person can go three minutes without air, three days without water, and three weeks without food. It's doubtful that anyone is going to suffocate at elk camp. Starvation is highly unlikely as well. And while dying of thirst may be possible under bizarre circumstances, it's hard to imagine water deprivation as a serious threat to an elk hunter. However, ensuring a safe and sufficient supply of water is a pertinent issue in planning for an elk camp. Rationing water or, worse still, becoming ill from a contaminated water source are needless calamities that can be avoided with a little advance planning.

The first step in ensuring a sufficient supply of water is assessing your demands. For personal consumption, it's possible to get by with as little as a gallon per day, per person. If a portion of fluid intake comes from other sources such as sport and soft drinks, milk, or juice, individuals might not even need a full gallon per day. But staying hydrated is important to

Staying hydrated while you hunt is critical, so having enough potable water in camp is a major priority.

Cooking demands a good deal of water, but it also calls for care not to waste water.

feeling good and maximizing physical performance, so it's wise to have plenty of liquids available.

Beyond drinking water, consider how much water you will use in cooking and washing dishes. Washing hands, hair, and showering also require considerable amounts of water. What are the expectations of camp members along those lines? And if you're using livestock, there must be an available water source for your animals, either natural or supplemented with stock water in camp.

I almost hate to offer estimations of water consumption, as needs vary so widely depending on the geographical and weather conditions at camp and individual expectations. That said, here are some figures to jumpstart your calculations. First, count on the aforementioned one gallon per person, per day for individual consumption. Add another gallon per person, per day for uses such as brushing teeth, washing dishes, and dousing the cook after a particularly bad meal. A hot shower requires around two to three gallons of water; washing hair can be done with a gallon or so. Based on those figures, a party of five that spends a week in camp can easily consume thirty-five to sixty gallons of water. Where will it come from?

Transporting Water from Home

The simplest solution is to transport water from home in containers. Water from a known source has a predictable taste and, more importantly, holds little danger of contamination from microbiological organisms that can cause illness. Plastic water containers designed for camping are typically inexpensive and hold five or six gallons. However, these reservoirs aren't particularly durable, so

Water is heavy stuff when you want to transport it, so keep that in mind when you start stuffing the truck.

Metal cream cans used for water storage containers.

care must be taken when packing them for transportation. They also tend to rupture on impact. I once dropped such a container while unloading it from the back of a pickup. A long split in the side ruined the jug and sent five gallons of water spewing in all directions—mainly toward my pant legs.

Much more durable, but also difficult to find, are old metal cream cans. These come in several sizes and can occasionally be found at a garage sale or purchased elsewhere. Even if the price seems high, don't hesitate to make the investment. Cream cans are easy to clean and with reasonable care will outlast their owners. We still use ten-gallon cream cans for water storage in our camp that were acquired over two decades ago.

Plastic food-grade jugs or barrels that may have originally been used to store cooking liquids for restaurants and other commercial food services are another serviceable option. These units often have a capacity of five to thirty gallons and are quite durable. Some come with a spigot that makes it possible to place them on a stand for easy pouring. Just make sure they're thoroughly cleaned so your water doesn't taste like the container's original substance.

While bringing water from home is often the simplest way to supply your camp, there are some drawbacks. Water is heavy. At eight pounds per gallon, fifty gallons weighs around four hundred pounds—a considerable load to add to a vehicle that's already burdened with other camp gear. Bulk is another factor: fifty gallons of water takes up a significant amount of space.

Natural Water Sources

If a safe water source is available at or near camp, then bringing along enough empty containers to supply the camp for a couple of days is more practical than bringing water from home. Pitching camp at or near a developed campground, such as one operated by the Forest Service, generally provides handy access to water, but it's wise to check availability in advance as the water system may be shut down before the opening of elk season.

Backcountry outfitters usually rely on a natural spring for their water, which is another option for do-it-yourself elk camps. Springwater taken at its source in the ground is generally safe for human consumption, but some advance knowledge of the location and the purity of the source is necessary for complete confidence. Fecal contaminants from animals and humans sometimes infest natural water sources that appear to be perfectly clean and taste wonderful. Areas around streams, lakes, and springs with scat or other indications of animal use such as beaver ponds and browsed shrubbery might very well be contaminated with illness-causing microorganisms.

Developed campgrounds often provide a safe, reliable source of water.

There are a few things to keep in mind when storing water in camp, whether you bring it from home or haul it from a spring or creek. When the weather is warm, water stays cooler if you store it on the ground, covered with a tarp in a shady location. Extended cold periods can cause water to freeze in the containers. Avoid this inconvenience, which might split the sides of your containers, by moving the water into a heated tent. Cached along a sidewall away from the heating source, the water will remain unfrozen and cool. As a rule of thumb, water stored in large containers can handle outside nighttime temperatures in the upper twenties without freezing. If it gets much colder, move the containers inside.

Water Purification

If you need water but are unsure of its safety, several procedures can make water potable. Iodine tablets work fine, although you must wait a certain length of time after their use before drinking. Water temperature, pH level, and the amount of sediment in the water (cloudiness) all affect the ability of iodine to effectively kill microorganisms. And iodine does not kill *Cryptosporidium* cysts, which if ingested by humans, commonly spawn fever and an acute illness of the digestive system. Water treated with iodine is also not recommended for individuals with thyroid problems, pregnant women, or consumption extending beyond a few weeks.

The simplest way to purify water is to boil it.

A long-standing method of water purification involves boiling. Years ago, experts advised boiling water for at least two minutes to ensure its safety. Currently, the rule of thumb is to simply bring the water to a rolling boil. The time and temperature involved in achieving the boil will effectively kill any microorganisms. However, it is wise to increase boiling time at higher elevations. Above 6,500 feet, the Centers for Disease Control (CDC) recommends increasing the boiling time to three minutes. Although boiling kills microbes in the water, it doesn't remove sediment and it tends to give water a flat taste.

Water filters are another popular choice, particularly among backpackers. There are a variety of capacities and configurations, but all purifiers employ essentially the same technology. A pump, or suction from the mouth, forces water through a filter with microscopic pores that are too small for microorganisms to pass through provided your filter is actually designed for removing microbes.

The CDC recommends that filters capable of removing the two most common parasitic cysts have a pore size of one micron. As the cysts are larger than two microns, this ensures that they will be unable to pass through the filter. However, it's important that your filter have an *absolute* rather than *nominal* pore size of one micron. An absolute pore size is the largest the filter can possibly contain. A nominal pore size simply refers to an average. A filter with a nominal pore size of one micron might contain pores large enough for cysts to pass through.

Another way to purify water is to use a purifier, usually one that incorporates fine-particle filters.

The CDC also notes that filters labeled with any one of the following statements are designed to remove cysts: "Reverse osmosis," "Tested and certified by NSF Standard 53 or 58 for cyst removal," and "Tested and certified by NSF Standard 53 or 58 for cyst reduction." Filters labeled as, "One-micron filter," "Effective against Giardia," or "EPA approved" may not provide adequate protections.

For instance, the "one-micron filter" may be a nominal measurement, not an absolute measurement. A filter that is "effective against Giardia" may not filter smaller illness-causing cysts. The fact that a filter is "EPA approved" says nothing, as the EPA does not test, approve, or register filters based on their effectiveness in removing microbes.

In general, filters sold for household use, like the water-pitcher type kept in many refrigerators, are not manufactured for microbe removal and won't be suitable for hunting or camping. Look for a filter from a sporting goods or backpacking store specifically designed for outdoor water purification.

Although properly designed filters effectively eliminate microbiological contaminants, improper use may lead to illness. Waterborne microbes can live in sufficient numbers to cause illness in very small quantities of water. Drops on the intake hose and water that remains in the hose after use still have the same properties as water from the source that is being filtered. The only water that is safe to drink is that which has passed through the filter. Thus, you must make sure that your filtered water isn't contaminated by untreated water on your hands or anywhere on your container.

Once, my family accompanied another couple on a summer backpacking trip. My friend's wife meticulously filtered their water from a source that we had previously used in its natural state. No one got sick, of course, but it wasn't due to her purification technique. After pumping water, she crammed the intake and output hoses from the filter into the same plastic bag, effectively contaminating the output hose—and whatever water container it supplied—with the unfiltered droplets on the input hose.

Why Purify?
Boiling, chemically treating, or filtering water can be a real pain. But the illnesses caused by untreated water are exceedingly more

painful. Protozoan cysts, bacteria, and viruses are all potentially present in surface water, and other places like shallow wells, and represent very real threats to uninformed or careless hunters.

The two most common protozoan cysts that routinely sicken outdoor folks are *Giardia lamblia* and *Cryptosporidium,* single-cell parasites with a relatively hard, outside shell. The hardened shell is what makes *Cryptosporidium* difficult to kill with chemical treatments like iodine and chlorine, although a fairly new product called Aqua Mira, which contains chlorine dioxide, is advertised as effectively killing the cysts. Also, *Crypto* cysts typically range from two to five microns, while those that produce giardiasis are five to fifteen microns. Just how small is a micron? One millionth of a meter (.0000394 inches). So if you think you might purify water by straining it through a recycled tea bag or coffee filter, forget it.

Although the symptoms of infection vary somewhat, giardiasis and cryptosporidiosis—the names commonly associated with the illnesses—affect the intestinal tract. Once an animal or human ingests cysts, these invaders live in the digestive tract and are passed in the stool. A single stool from an infected human or animal can contain millions of cysts. Due to their protective outer shell, the cysts can survive in feces, soil, water, and other areas for extended periods of time.

Symptoms take some time to develop. *Crypto* commonly results in watery diarrhea, fever, stomach cramps, nausea, and vomiting. Symptoms typically appear in two to ten days and may last up to two weeks. Giardiasis causes diarrhea, gas, stomach cramps, nausea, and greasy stools. These symptoms usually appear in one to two weeks. Persistence of a month or longer is not uncommon.

Thankfully, cryptosporidiosis and giardiasis can be treated with drugs that markedly shorten the duration of the painful symptoms.

But because of the delay between ingestion of cysts and the appearance of symptoms, especially with giardiasis, many people incorrectly diagnose their discomfort and delay treatment. If you experience any of the symptoms associated with these two parasites during or after your time in elk camp, contact a physician. The doctor will likely request a stool sample to check for cysts.

While cyst infections are among the most common causes of illness due to the ingestion of untreated water, bacterial infections of the type routinely associated with food poisoning (e.g., *E. coli*, and salmonella) may also originate in water. Filters, boiling, and chemical treatments are all typically effective in eliminating bacterial contaminants.

Viral illnesses might also be possible. However, as the viruses that invade humans are short-lived and would probably reach a backcountry environment only by a human carrier, the odds of contracting a viral illness via water are exceedingly small.

The prospect of becoming acutely ill in elk camp due to a waterborne microbe can be unsettling, but it's relatively simple to ensure the purity of your water. In the fifty years my family has maintained an elk camp, no one has gotten sick due to water contaminants. Bad cooking is another story.

— 9 —

EXTREME WEATHER

Easing slowly through a broad expanse of heavy timber, I spot an elk just ahead in the lodge poles. Two things are immediately obvious: it's a big bull and it's alert, ready to run.

I've already filled my tag, but my companion hasn't. Motioning to Doug behind me, I point out the bull and tell him to shoot—quickly. He raises his rifle and fires. Down goes the elk and up go our gloved hands in happy salute to our good fortune.

In an hour the meat is fully boned and carefully wrapped in two pieces of the hide, which we weight with rocks to keep scavengers at bay. We saw the six-tined antlers from the elk's skull then undertake a few minutes' oral surgery to extract the ivories. Job finished, we turn upslope to begin the two-mile hike back to camp.

It's midafternoon by the time we arrive. An inviting aroma in the cook tent reminds me that I haven't eaten a proper lunch. As I settle into a bowl of creamy white beans and tender ham, Uncle Tom asks when we plan to pack the elk.

"Tomorrow morning," I reply, explaining that the mule had more than a workout packing two animals yesterday and that I'd like to give her a day of rest.

"Don't think I'd wait," he observes. "The weather's a-changing. Haven't you noticed the wind?"

I hadn't. Poking my head out of the cook tent, I immediately sense that he's right. A slight, but steady breeze is rising from the north. Though the sky is blue, it's obvious a front is moving in our direction. By the time I finish my beans, Tom has the packsaddle on the reluctant mule. And by nightfall Doug's bull is in camp.

The next morning we awaken to a steady rain that soon turns to enormous wet snowflakes. The ground around camp is sodden with moisture. With a shudder I imagine the condition of the steep trail we traversed yesterday to retrieve the elk. Thanks to the foresight of my wise uncle, we've dodged a miserable and potentially dangerous encounter with bad weather.

Drenching rain, heavy snow, high winds, and extreme cold can quickly transform an idyllic hunt into a test of human will and survival skills. Yet with good equipment and proper response to changing conditions, a well-crafted elk camp can weather the worst that nature has to offer. Here's how to handle the most common challenges brought on by changing weather.

Rain

I'd rather deal with cold and snow at elk camp than rain. Frozen ground isn't normally a problem for pack animals or vehicles, but wet, slick mud certainly is. Unfortunately, in the course of transforming from balmy to blustery, Mother Nature often throws in a good downpour, sometimes a hard, steady rain that can soak an entire camp and the spirits of its occupants.

With a dry place to pass a rainy spell, though, a drenching rain isn't nearly so dismal. Protecting your gear from a soaking also reduces the discomfort. To that end, the first order of business is to keep the interior of your tent(s) dry.

A good tent fly is the best defense against rain. For maximum protection, make sure the fly extends a couple of feet beyond the eaves of the tent. This helps protect the walls from rain driven at an angle by the wind. It also keeps the dripline away from the bottom of the tent, where water running down from the roof can quickly soak into the interior. If your fly isn't large enough to extend beyond the eaves, create a temporary overhang by sliding small tarps or heavy plastic garbage bags under the fly and attaching them to the guylines that support the sidewalls.

It also helps to shovel a berm of dirt against the outside bottom of the tent walls. Pile the dirt on the sod cloth—the flap of material sewn to the bottom of the sidewall—or if the sod cloth is turned to the interior, simply bank dirt against the walls. If you disturb soil with living plants to create the berm, make sure you replace it when you break camp.

With a good fly and a banked tent, the interior should stay dry. However, you'll likely have gear to protect that you don't want to store inside. Whether you're camped in the backcountry or at roadside, it's a good idea to bring along a few small poly tarps that can be thrown over the woodpile, hay and tack, chainsaw and gas cans, and other items you need to protect from the rain.

Heavy Snow

In some cases, the transition from rain to heavy snow is but a matter of a few hours. At other times the snow comes on the heels of a cold front, swirling in on frigid tendrils long after the temperature has plunged below freezing.

A thick blanket of white is no threat to the occupants of a wall tent, as long as the tent can hold the extra weight. But a heavy covering of wet snow adds a staggering load to a tent. Heaped on the typical twelve-by-fourteen-foot wall tent, a foot of moisture-rich snow can add the weight of a bull elk to the frame. An inadequate frame will collapse, potentially injuring the tent's occupants—not to mention the inconvenience of reconstructing a flattened tent.

Anyone who has spent time in the Rockies knows how fast a squall can come upon you. Sun one day, snow the next.

Several precautions will protect your camp against such an occurrence. If the snow comes in the daytime or the waking hours of darkness, reduce the tent's load by regularly clearing the roof. A tent fly of slick material makes this much easier because sometimes snow will slide from the fly on its own, depending on the roof pitch. If not, push out on the roof from the inside in a bouncing motion to slide snow down the roof and off the eaves.

If you expect a heavy snow load to accumulate at night or when the camp is unattended, it's a good idea to add some additional support to the frame. The ridgepole carries the heaviest load, so start here. For wooden frames and internal frames made of pipe, add a wood post that runs from ground to ridgepole at or near the center of the tent. A four-inch-diameter post is adequate. Measure from the bottom of the ridgepole to the ground, and then add about an inch. You will have to lift the ridgepole slightly to install the post, but the additional weight will keep it in place. Cut a shallow V-notch in the smaller end of the post to further secure it to the ridgepole.

A similar procedure can be used to reinforce the eave poles that support the sidewalls. If the sidewalls are supported by stakes, the weight of the snow will be distributed more evenly rather than by a single pole. Good sidewall stakes aren't likely to break under a load of heavy snow. However, if the guylines are loose the stakes may twist out of position, leaving a sagging sidewall. When the snow starts drifting down, check the tension on the guylines and tighten any that are loose.

A slick fly helps to shed a heavy snow load.

Sometimes you might want to add a center pole to your ridgepole, to accommodate a heavy snow load.

High Winds

Howling winds have given me more bad nights in elk camp than any other weather hazard. Beyond the annoyance, a gale can flatten a poorly secured tent or tear a loose fly to pieces.

Tight, strong guylines are a tent's best protection in high winds. To prepare for a big blow, evaluate the ground stakes and guylines on all four sides. At least three guylines should run from the ends of the tent: one from the ridgepole and two from the eaves at the corners of the sidewalls. For an extra measure of protection, attach an extra guyline to the ridgepole. If you double the guylines on the ridgepole, locate their ground stakes about six feet apart to form a V with the point terminating at the ridgepole. And check the ropes that hold the fly on the tent to make sure they're tight. If the wind starts whipping an unsecured section of the fly, it can tear or fray even high-quality fabric.

Also assess the security of gear stored outside. Wind can carry things like empty water containers, loose hay, and saddle blankets a long distance. Tarps covering gear can be whisked away as well unless they're tightly secured. Weight them down with chunks of wood or other heavy objects or temporarily cache them on the sheltered side of the tent or in the back of a pickup.

You can also add doubled guylines to the ridgepole for extra support in high wind.

Freezing Temperatures

Certain destinations make for cold camping any time of year. On several occasions I've hunted elk near the northwest boundary of Yellowstone National Park in mid-November. Cold settles completely into the high basins and creek bottoms in the area, often pushing nighttime temperatures in Gallatin River drainages to below zero during hunting season.

With a good woodburning stove for heat, passing a week in such weather can be surprisingly pleasant—if you have enough wood to keep the stove burning. It's much easier to stack a supply of firewood before a big chill settles over the mountains, so always make sure your camp has plenty on hand.

Pitching a camp in very cold conditions can be miserable. If you have the slightest inkling that you might encounter wintry weather, bring along a supply of firewood from home so that a stove can be stoked as soon as the tent is raised.

Keeping the stove burning through the night is essential in frigid temperatures unless you want to awaken to frost on the inside of your tent. Large-capacity stoves filled with good quality wood typically burn all night with their dampers closed. Small stoves, such as those used in backcountry camps, require some tending. On one occasion when faced with very cold nights and a small stove, I set an alarm to rouse me once during the night to stoke the stove. It's not much fun to crawl out of a toasty sleeping bag at 2 A.M. to poke more wood on the fire, but it's less fun to wake up four hours later to a cold stove and freezing tent.

Food storage poses another challenge in very cold weather. Most perishable foods such as fruits and vegetables must be protected from freezing. Canned goods, drinks, and any other foodstuffs that contain liquid must be kept from freezing as well. When temperatures drop

(Opposite page) When the wind is whipping and it's nine degrees, don't go far for your firewood — stack it right outside the tent.

The camp thermometer showing nine degrees Fahrenheit. Ah, elk weather.

In really cold conditions, bring your coolers into the wall tent and put them next to an outer wall; they'll stay cool.

to around twenty-five degrees Fahrenheit at night but warm above freezing during the day, food can be kept "refrigerated" in coolers outdoors without danger of freezing. In lower temperatures, keep items you don't want to freeze in coolers stored inside the tent along the wall farthest from the stove. Place water containers in a similar location.

Extreme cold and other weather hazards can crop up nearly anywhere worth pitching an elk camp. With reasonable preparation, these conditions aren't really too tough on hunters and make for lasting memories. "Remember that time it got down to fifteen below and we had eleven inches of snow on the ground…" makes a great opening line to a camp story. Preparing yourself ahead of time is the best way to ensure the tale has a happy ending.

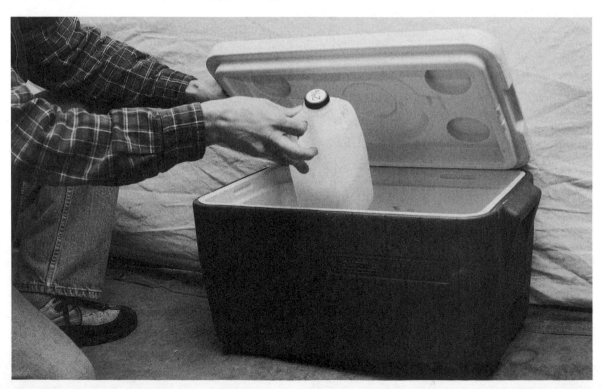

— 10 —

CAMPING IN BEAR COUNTRY

Folks hunt elk for a variety of reasons. Some seek solitude, an escape from milling crowds, screeching cell phones, and traffic congestion. Others, especially in rural areas and small towns closer to hunting grounds, are in it for the meat—an elk will keep a family of four in lean, protein-rich entrees well beyond winter.

Bears frequent elk country for many of the same reasons. Grizzlies kill and consume elk, especially the very young and very old of the species. Along with their black-coated cousins, lean grizzlies fresh from a winter's sleep also clean up the carcasses of elk that starve in winter. And in many prime hunting areas, both species of bear scavenge elk carcasses and gut piles left in the wild by successful hunters.

Bears typically love solitude. Aside from unfortunate animals that are habituated to human sources of food, bears don't mix well with civilization. Confronted with a hiker, hunter, or automobile, most bears retreat to more private haunts. Grizzlies are especially averse to human society—it's no coincidence that our largest predator most frequently inhabits wilderness areas and other remote locations where encounters with our kind are minimal.

When planning and using their camps, elk hunters must keep several things in mind. First, elk camps bring humans right into the heart of bear habitat. Second, bears feed most actively in the fall, constantly seeking high-quality nutrition to put on fat reserves before entering their dens for hibernation. Research indicates that black bears may lose up to 40 percent of their body weight during hibernation, so they must bulk up before retiring underground for their long winter's nap. Finally,

A sow grizzly and an older cub. A mama bear who fears for her young becomes a most dangerous bear.

and obviously, the food and fresh meat commonly found in an elk camp are potential attractants to bears.

When bears enter a camp, most often in search of food they've smelled, a number of outcomes are possible—all negative. A well-fed bear may simply prowl around camp while hunters are in the field, sniffing at unfamiliar items before leaving. While no direct conflict occurs in this situation, it still represents an incident that may habituate the bear to humans and possibly lead to a more serious confrontation later on.

A more serious scenario that sometimes occurs when hunters are away from camp involves a bear that smells food inside a tent and rips open the canvas to investigate. From there, the hungry bruin often tears into containers, packs, and cooking gear. Returning hunters discover a trashed camp and may blame the bear for the problem, even though the animal was only pursuing a very natural course of autumn behavior.

If hunters return to surprise a marauding bear in camp or if a bear invades a camp when hunters are present, the consequences may be severe. If the bear stands its ground to defend what it perceives as a food source it's already claimed, or hazing efforts by hunters fail to repel the invading bruin, the confrontation may escalate to the point where the bear gets shot, perhaps after injuring someone.

This outcome would be truly unfortunate. A bear mauling is one of the worst experiences imaginable to the average outdoorsman. But the unnecessary killing of a bear is also tragic. In the contiguous United States, where grizzlies are relatively rare, such a loss diminishes the wild character of the landscapes most cherished by hunters.

Thankfully, the odds of a destructive human-bear encounter in elk camp are very low. You are more likely to be injured in a collision with a deer or elk while driving to camp than by a bear in camp. By taking some reasonable precautions when camping in bear country, those odds can be driven even lower.

Choosing Safe Campsites

As any hunter knows, animals leave indications of their presence even when they can't be seen. Fresh scat, claw marks on trees, overturned rocks, and torn logs may indicate that a bear is frequenting an area. If you find such a sign near your intended campsite and feel that it was made recently, relocate to a different spot.

Avoid areas that might be especially attractive to bears in the fall. Moist, low-lying bottoms along creeks or near springs often support

HANDLING HORSE FEED

Livestock feed and pet food should be considered bear attractants and handled accordingly. Hay and whole oats are better choices for horse and mule feeds in bear country than pellets or grain mixes (sweet feeds), which include sweeteners that are like candy to bears. Dog food typically contains meat byproducts and/or oils that are highly odorous and very attractive to bears.

Feed for stock animals is a major bear attractant and must be secured

undergrowth and berry-bearing shrubs such as chokecherries and huckleberries, which are highly favored by bruins. Camping in more open areas, rather than dense stands of timber, gives hunters and bears greater visibility, reducing the potential for a surprise encounter. If you see evidence of garbage, fish entrails, or other items left behind by a previous camp, find a different place to pitch your own camp.

In short, use common sense to locate your camp in a spot that's unlikely to bring bears to your tent.

How Not to Invite a Bear for Breakfast

The majority of bear incidents in camp involve food. Black and grizzly bears are opportunistic omnivores that are all too happy to consume any food prepared by humans—and a lot of things not consumed by humans, such as grubs, earthworms, and rotting elk ribs. A bear's nose is its most highly developed sense organ, and a cruising bruin can detect food odors from an incredible distance. With these factors in mind, the principles of food storage in bear country are: first, eliminate or reduce food odors as much as possible; and second, store food and odoriferous garbage where it can't be reached by bears.

Canned goods or foods sealed in glass jars don't emit odors. Until opened, they aren't likely to attract a bear. Cans and jars become more problematic as garbage after the food has been consumed. Foods packaged in plastic, like pasta, trail mix, and dried fruits, are more likely to smell. One way to reduce any odors is to place food in large sealable plastic food-storage bags and then in heavy garbage bags. Frozen or chilled meats can be treated likewise before going into coolers.

In some locations where bear populations are high or there has been a history of problems with bears in camps, common sense or government regulations may dictate specific food storage, consumption, and disposal procedures to keep human food inaccessible to roaming bears. This includes caching food in bear-proof containers.

Roadside camps offer more options for food storage than backcountry camps. Storing food inside a vehicle, either in the cab or in a pickup topper, is a generally accepted method of bear-proofing by the Forest Service, even though bears have damaged automobiles attempting to reach food stored inside. If you keep food in a vehicle, make sure that the doors and windows are tightly closed to reduce odors and prevent bears from finding a "clawhold" that might give them access to the interior. Storage boxes constructed from special plastics, metal, or wood with metal reinforcement may also meet government regulations for bear-proof storage. However, with the exception of specially manufactured—and expensive—plastic storage units made especially for food storage in bear country, these containers are too heavy to be useful for anything but drive-up camps.

At backcountry camps or in situations where other storage options are unavailable,

Most places where grizzlies roam are posted with notices about safe food storage.

A lockable, tight-fitting metal storage box can serve as bear-proof storage, as long as a bear can't peel back a lid edge.

Be sure to position storage containers on a bear pole far enough away from trees that the bear can climb.

the backpacker's practice of suspending food well above the ground is the simplest way to keep food safe. As a general rule, items must be elevated at least ten feet above the ground to keep them out of reach of an adult grizzly standing on its hind legs. Experts also recommend that food be stored a minimum of one hundred yards from your camp.

At campsites that see regular use, folks with a long-term perspective in mind may fasten a "bear pole" about twelve feet up between two trees. Like tent poles, the best bear poles come from standing dead timber with a minimum diameter of four inches. Check the length of the pole on the ground before hefting it up, and then wedge it between stout branches and the trunk of each tree or fasten it with nails. Once the bear pole is in place, tie a stick, rock, or weighted stuff sack to the end of the rope and toss it over. Then hoist up the covered food items and tie off the rope.

You can also substitute a length of heavy rope for the wooden pole. Use sisal rope or a nonstretching nylon so the load won't sag down far enough for a bear to reach. To be safe, tie the rope about thirteen feet above the ground in both trees. Small pulleys, fastened to the heavy rope before it's tied in the trees, will make it easier to hoist items from the ground—just be sure to thread your small hoisting ropes through the pulleys first.

Another option for bear-proof food storage that utilizes rope and two trees is what I call the "raising M" method. Loop one end of a long rope over a tree branch about twelve feet above the ground, either by climbing the tree or pitching the rope over the branch with a weighted object. Tie the end of the rope that is not weighted to the bottom of the tree or another anchoring point at ground level. Then pull the excess rope over the branch and let it coil on the ground halfway between the two trees. Now loop the weighted end of the rope over a branch on the second tree at approximately the same height as the first, making sure the rope is long enough to reach the ground between the trees. At this point, the rope should form a loose "M" as it snakes over the branch of one tree, back down to the ground in the center, and over a branch of the second tree.

To elevate food with this setup, tie the bags or storage containers to the rope at ground level at the center between the two trees. Then pull the rope from either end to elevate the load in the middle by "raising the M." When the load is at the desired height, tie off the rope ends to tree branches or other anchors. If you're hanging the food alone, secure the rope at one end of the M before raising the load. Just be sure the load is fastened to the rope in such a way that it can slide to remain centered between the trees.

> ### BEAR POLE ROPES
>
> Lightweight cord is sufficient for suspending food, except when you need to support multiple items between two trees. And it is more portable than heavier ropes. One hundred feet of parachute cord or 3/16-inch braided nylon rope will do. If you're camping with livestock, ropes for packing can also be used to hoist food items.

In some camping areas, you might be lucky enough to find a natural bear pole in the form of an unobstructed tree branch, a leaning tree, or a dead tree that has fallen against a living tree with its top leaning away. Simply toss a rope over the branch or tree trunk and hoist the load up to the desired height. Remember that black and grizzly bears are proficient climbers, so hang the food at least four feet away from the trunk of the tree.

Handling Garbage

Garbage is often more likely to lure a bear into camp than the food stored in its original container. Take sardines or canned spam, for example. Sealed up in its tin, neither emits a strong odor. Peel back

An obvious grizzly — note the pig-like nose, humped back, wide face, and ginger tipped hair.

the lid, though, and watch out. Even your campmates in the next tent will know what you're eating. If other people can catch a whiff of your snack, what about a bear?

Yet even the smelliest food items won't necessarily increase the likelihood of a bear in camp if handled properly. Be careful not to drip or otherwise transfer juices or oil onto clothing or other gear, as the smell may remain on the item for days.

Once the container has been emptied, treat the garbage just as you would food. Garbage is best stored in doubled, heavy-duty garbage bags. But it's helpful to first reduce the amount of garbage in camp, and its accompanying odors, by "treating" it with fire. Burnable food containers will be completely consumed by a hot fire. And the fat, oil, and juices that cling to metal cans can be burned away in a fire before they're placed in garbage bags and hung from a tree or stored in a bear-proof container. Some campers use paper plates and bowls so that these can be burned after a meal.

Cooking and Cleaning Up

The basic rule for food consumption—avoid transferring smells to clothing and other gear—also holds for cooking and kitchen cleanup. In backcountry situations where food is stored by elevating it, it is best to cook near the food storage area, downwind and at least one hundred yards from the sleeping tent. This concentrates food odors in one location, away from where you'll be sleeping. It may be difficult to judge prevailing wind patterns in unfamiliar country, but one general principle applies everywhere: at night, when your camp is most vulnerable to a bear approaching undetected, air currents generally move downhill. Thus, the best location for your tent is uphill of the place where you'll be cooking.

No matter how primitive or elaborate your camp, the same care should be taken when cooking. Frying meats with high fat content, such as bacon or beef steaks, will almost certainly send grease spattering in all directions, as will stir-frying vegetables or meat in hot oil. A better alternative is a portable gas grill. While you cook, grease will be contained on the inside of the covered grill, which can then be fired at its highest temperature for a while to burn away lingering odors. Fish or meat cooked over an open fire should be first wrapped in foil. After the meal, simply burn the foil in a hot campfire.

Try to reduce lingering odor during all food preparation. Chopping, slicing, kneading, and other common kitchen tasks should be undertaken on hard, nonporous surfaces like plastic instead of material that will more readily absorb juices and odors, such as wood. Wipe up with paper towels instead of cloth and burn the paper when you're finished.

The food you eat also plays a role in controlling odor. For example, pasta sauce in a jar requires less preparation time and is far less likely to create lingering odors than cooking your own. Transferring foods from their original containers into heavy-duty, zip-top bags allows you to reseal the bags after use, further reducing potential odors.

Try to use as few pots and pans as possible when cooking—the fewer there are to clean up, the lower the possibility of spreading odors.

As with food preparation, paper towels are handy for after-meal cleaning because they can be burned. Before you wash them in soapy water, thoroughly wipe your cookware and utensils with paper towels to trap food particles, oil, and grease. Then promptly burn the paper. Scents lingering in dirty dishwater can be reduced by pouring the water carefully around the outer edge of a hot fire, where residue will be consumed by the heat. Store the clean dish-pans and cookware in a bear-proof location.

No single procedure or set of procedures will make your elk camp totally immune to bears. However, by taking simple, common-sense precautions, chances are you'll retire from elk hunting without ever having to banish a bear from camp.

— 11 —

KEEPING LIVESTOCK

The object of ferrying all the gear required to create an elk camp is, of course, hunting. While nearly everyone has visited the age-old fantasy of shooting a bull from a folding chair in camp, wapiti seldom fall within shouting range of the cook tent. More often than not, the best hunting is found miles from the nearest roads and trails, putting your quarry at a considerable distance from the nearest vehicle access.

If you're in reasonably good physical condition, hunting a couple of hours from camp isn't too taxing. But suppose you down a bull that far from camp? How will you get hundreds of pounds of meat, not to mention the hide and antlers, back to camp?

Dragging is one option. My older brother and I once pulled the quarters of a cow elk into camp from a distant meadow. I'll not do that again—ever. Boning a critter and packing it in a backpack beats the heck out of lugging one for any distance. But folks who routinely back-pack elk from the mountains go home a couple inches shorter than the height indicated on their driver's license—intense spinal compression is tough on your physique and posture.

The best way to transport elk to camp is to let, or persuade, someone else to do it for you. But as you'll only convince a fellow human to pack your elk once, a strong horse or mule is a more reliable choice. The hundreds of dollars the weekend cowboy sinks into feed, vet bills, and shoeing over the course of a year will seem a bargain when there's an 800-pound bull on yonder mountainside that needs moving to camp.

They might be ornery, but pack mules are a big help to the elk hunter.

Containment Methods

If you're fortunate enough to use livestock as part of your elk-hunting experience, you'll need to make some accommodations for them in camp, preferably something that's humane to the livestock and easy on the landscape.

No matter how you handle your stock in camp, it's a good idea for them to experience similar containment ahead of time, at home. Hobbles, pickets, and portable electric fences are all excellent for restricting the movement of horses and mules in camp. However, a mule that's never been picketed may tangle itself in the rope and become seriously injured if left unattended. And a young mare that has never been stung by an electric fence at home might bolt right through the wire at camp if spooked by a chainsaw being fired up.

Which brings up another relevant point in avoiding a livestock disaster in elk camp: bring only the necessary number of steady, experienced animals.

Pack horses often take the place of mules. It all depends on what livestock are available.

Hitching rails are easy to make, and a very convenient way to tether your pack horses, but tough on tree roots and vegetation.

Traditional Tie-Ups

In some places, hunters still use the age-old practice of tying animals to trees or an improvised hitching rail. However, this is tough on the environment and must be terribly uncomfortable for horses and mules. How would you like to be tethered on a short rope for hours on end?

Highlines

Containing livestock on a highline—a strong rope strung between two trees—is a better method, both for your animals and nature. Halter ropes are attached to the highline, allowing animals some freedom of movement. This reduces pawing and soil damage and keeps hooves away from tree roots, which are often found just a few inches below ground.

To string a highline, locate two trees far enough apart to accommodate the number of animals you intend to tether. Instead of crowding more animals on a single line, spread them out on two or more highlines in different areas. This not only reduces their effect on the topsoil, but also the potential for problems between animals.

Use broad webbing straps around the trees at either end of the highline to minimize damage to tree trunks. Although tree bark may seem impervious to rope damage, it isn't. Abrasion and compression from ropes can weaken a tree's resistance to parasites and may also damage the cambium layer, which transports nourishment from the roots to the top of the tree. If you don't have webbing straps, wrap rope around the trunk several times to achieve a

similar effect. If possible, attach your highline to large-diameter trees, as the bark isn't as easily damaged.

Setting up a highline gives your livestock a bit more room to move while tethered than on a hitching rail or tied to trees.

Secure the highline between the two trees, slightly higher than the head of your tallest animal. Determine how far apart you'd like to keep your animals—fifteen to twenty feet is a good estimate—then attach halter ropes to the line so that they can't slide around on the rope. Loops tied in the highline before you attach it to the trees work well for this purpose. The highline should be pulled taut and checked periodically for sagging. A drooping line may allow horses or mules to get their heads or feet over it, which could cause an injury.

Also pay attention to how and where you halter your animals to the line. Halter ropes should be long enough to allow freedom of movement, but not so long that an animal can get its feet over the rope. Tether compatible animals together. Experience at home should tell you which animals get along the best. When mixing stock from different owners, a good rule of thumb is to separate mares by tying geldings or mules between them. If a particular animal routinely causes trouble with others, isolate it on the end of the line or put it on a separate highline.

When using a single gentle animal, you can further increase its range of movement by tying its halter rope to a loop that slides on the highline. Never do this with multiple animals, though, as a tangled mess of halter ropes, and possibly injured stock, is the inevitable result.

Spend the money for true electric cable for an electric fence, and avoid cheap wire.

Pole and Two-Rope Corrals

Highlines work very well, but there are some other options. Old-timers sometimes erected makeshift corrals from timbers they lashed together or nailed to trees. If there are enough standing dead poles in the area to create a corral, this is still a reasonable approach— if allowed by local livestock regulations. Well-broke animals can be held in a temporary corral made by stringing two ropes between trees. If you think you might use this method, be sure to bring enough rope along. It takes two hundred feet of rope to create a twenty-five-by-twenty-five-foot two-rope corral, which is probably about the minimum area needed for a single animal. It is often necessary to move a rope corral frequently to minimize soil and root damage unless it's located on hard or stony ground.

Portable Electric Fences

A modern and highly effective method of corralling livestock in camp is the portable electric fence. A variety of fence-charging units are currently available, some of which run on just two D-cell batteries. Yet they pack enough wallop to get the attention of the most recalcitrant mule.

Setting up an electric fence enclosure is easy—provided you have the right materials. Start with a portable charger, and then select plastic fence posts with pointed metal ends that look like large nails. Simply step on the posts to plant them in the ground. Removing them is just as easy when you want to change the location of the corral. Instead of cheap electric fence wire, invest a little more money in the cord or webbing with fine wire woven through nylon. These electric fence lines are much easier to wind up and move, and webbing provides extra visibility as well.

A portable electric fence can work very well for livestock that are used to such an enclosure.

Just like with other methods of livestock containment, make sure your animals are broke to electric fencing before you put them in this enclosure in camp. Horses and mules familiar with electric fencing generally give it so much respect that you could probably get away with stringing the wire on poles without actually charging it.

In some backcountry locations, hunters string an additional electric wire around their tents as extra insurance against marauding bears. That's fine, so long as you don't forget about it when you lurch from the tent at 2 A.M. to relieve a full bladder. But not to worry—that's a mistake you won't make twice.

Natural Grazing

Although highlines, corrals, and electric fences will do a fine job of containing your livestock, they probably won't allow them enough range or mobility to feed on their own. If your camp is located in an area of vehicle access, it's no problem to bring hay or other feed along from home. In backcountry locations, though, you'll probably want your stock to obtain most of their ration from the range, perhaps supplemented with pellets or grain.

Make sure that your horses will like what you're going to feed them in camp. Give them a sample before you leave home.

Most outfitters use one or more methods to contain stock eating natural forage. One approach is to turn all but a few riding horses loose, then round up the stock as needed. Some, or all, of the loose animals should be outfitted with bells to help identify their location if they wander. Unfortunately, unless your horses are easy to catch and you're sure the lot won't hightail it to the trailer, you may waste hours chasing livestock that you'd rather spend hunting.

Hobbles and Pickets

Another technique that allows horses and mules to graze yet limits wandering is the use of hobbles. Livestock hobbled around the front legs have plenty of mobility for grazing, but will probably stick close to camp. Keep in mind that some animals become adept at traveling hobbled and can cover more distance overnight than you might think possible. If

LIVESTOCK FEEDS

When feeding horses and mules prepared feeds such as hay, grain, or pellets, don't forget that their needs in camp may be different from those at home. To the best of my knowledge, certified weed-free hay is required on public lands nationwide. Even if it isn't, that's what you should be using, as the spread of exotic weeds is one of the greatest threats to elk habitat. Before hitting the backcountry, feed your animals a weed-free ration for a day or two to clean their systems of any weed seeds.

If your animals are on pasture, make sure they like the prepared feed you're planning to use in camp. For example, our best mule hates alfalfa, preferring grass hay or native pasture. She isn't fond of hay cubes, but takes a sweetened grain mix (sweet feed) with relish. You can take the tough guy "let 'em get hungry enough and they'll eat it" attitude, but your animals will work harder and keep easier if they have access to adequate amounts of high-quality feed that they enjoy eating.

True weed-free hay — the only hay to use for feed in wilderness lands — comes with a certification tag.

you decide to hobble your horses, make sure they're introduced to the hobbles at home, before you slap them on in camp.

Picket ropes are a third option. Typically, some form of picket pin is driven into the ground. This might be a wooden stake that you cut from dead timber or a metal stake designed especially for this purpose. A length of rope connects the animal to the stake, typically by a front leg.

If you let your horses graze loose, only do so knowing they won't wander far, or you'll waste time chasing them.

Like hobbles, you must educate your animals to picketing at home before bringing them to camp.

Pickets must be carefully attended. Shod horses and mules can do considerable damage to meadow vegetation if left too long in one place. Their hooves generate high pressure, which is compounded by metal shoes. As vegetation typically rejuvenates slowly at high elevations, damage from over-picketed areas can last for years.

There is another practical reason for frequently moving picketed livestock: a hungry animal can quickly consume the forage from an area. A good rule of thumb for moving stock on pickets is to observe the vegetation around the picket. When you can see a ring forming, it's time for a move.

Watering Stock

In addition to containing and feeding your stock, you must provide access to water. Ideally, your camp will be next to a water source for your animals, but that's not always possible. The nearest surface water to our camp is about a half-mile away, making a trek to the spring to water the stock a daily chore.

If you are using a natural water source, you must also consider the environmental impact of watering your animals. Hoofed animals trampling the same stream bank can cause significant damage in a fairly short period of time.

This damage often occurs when dirt is knocked into the stream or vegetation along the bank is uprooted, promoting erosion. In either case, excess sediment enters the water. Mountain streams are often prime spawning areas for fish like cutthroat trout, and this

Take care to water livestock in rocky places where their hooves won't knock soil into the stream.

Your livestock often make your elk hunt a lot easier, so treat them as well as you'd treat yourself (saying you were a mule).

increased sedimentation can pollute the clean gravel they need to reproduce. Watering livestock away from steep banks of topsoil is important in maintaining stream health. Try to find a gravelly area with a gently sloped bank that will minimize the impact of your livestock on the stream environment.

Whether you pack the entire camp into the backcountry with livestock or pitch your tents near a road, horses and mules can greatly enhance the hunting experience. As the livestock often do more work than the humans, give them the best possible care while in camp—that's the request I read in the gentle brown eyes of Molly, my brother's twenty-three-year-old pet mule. Could a face like that lie?

— 12 —

CAMPMATES

While a well-furnished camp contributes to pleasurable elk hunting, in the grand scheme of things, *who* comes to camp is more important than what sort of a camp you set up. Among good-humored folks of like mind, minor accidents, inconveniences, and all those other experiences that lend color to camping and hunting yield nothing but merriment and fond memories. But stir a few intense, rigid personalities into the elk-camp cookpot, and it can be quite the opposite. Contentiousness, differing expectations, and incompatibility may do more than just yield unpleasant days in camp; they have the potential to sour friendships and family relationships long after the last pound of gear has been loaded for the trip home.

Predicting exactly who will get along is an inexact science. I've seen people of widely differing ages, political persuasions, income levels, and education become great friends in camp. At other times I've observed people you would expect to form an instant bond remain estranged for an entire hunt. As in marriage, though, shared values and life experience typically lead to the most harmonious relationships. Here are a few things to consider when you are recruiting bodies for elk camp.

Politics

Every other fall the opening of Montana's elk season falls within weeks of Election Day. Advocates for each major party are certain that their platforms and candidates are sure to save the nation from impending depression, war, moral collapse, and so on.

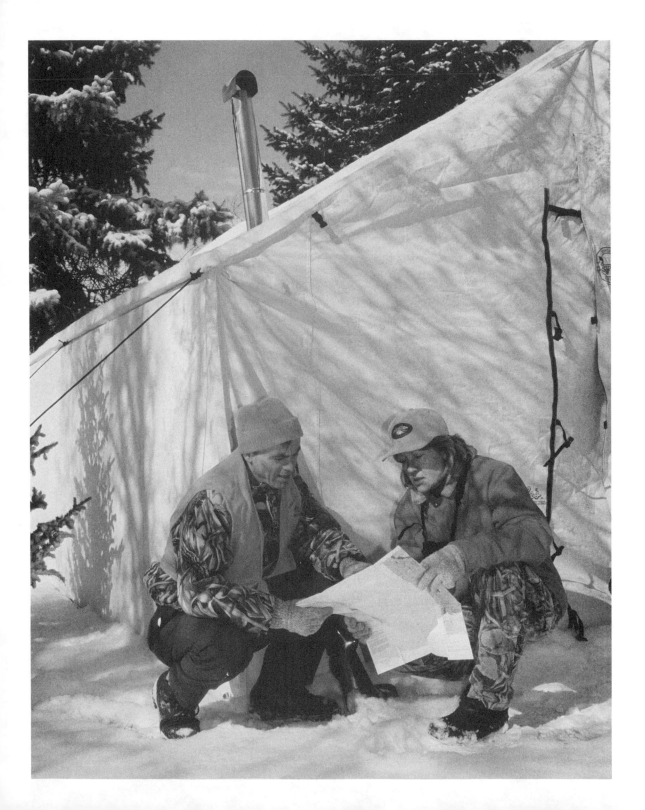

Having folks of different political persuasions in camp isn't necessarily a bad thing. But hard-headed, opinionated folks who don't know when to back away from a political discussion can spell disaster in the close quarters of elk camp. Do you really think you're going to change someone else's political opinion in a heated debate in a crowded wall tent?

The best way to avoid potential conflicts spawned by politics and other social issues is to cut the conversation short before things escalate. I once shared camp with a lone "wolf lover" among a bunch of "wolf haters." The few times the anti-wolf fellows started in on the subject the man kept his mouth shut. He did this out of respect for camp harmony, and he also probably sensed that no debate was winnable in that crowd. Six days later we all parted company in peace.

With all of the positive things to discuss after dinner, there is really no reason to raise your—or anyone else's—blood pressure with a divisive point of view that will create disruption.

Expectations

My dad and his two brothers formed the nucleus of our family's elk camp in the fledgling years. Five decades later, cousins, grandsons, sons-in-law, and friends all make the annual pilgrimage to our encampment.

Everyone generally gets along just fine, but over the years we've had our share of disagreements and hard feelings, just like any family. From my vantage point, most of the conflict has been the result of differing expectations.

Let's face it—planning, pitching, and maintaining a traditional elk camp involves plenty of work and expense. And those two aspects—

(Opposite page) Teamwork is essential to a successful elk hunt. Never underestimate the smarts or talents of your campmates.

Check and double-check your equipment list. You'll always end up needing that thing you almost forgot.

work and expense—are most likely the cause of the differing but uncommunicated expectations that lead to dissatisfaction and conflict.

Planning

Somewhere along the line, our family instituted an annual planning meeting about six weeks prior to the hunting trip to hammer out responsibilities and expectations. Ideally, everyone attending the camp makes the meeting, but that isn't always possible. At a minimum, the fellows ramrodding the expedition get together for a few hours to map out the essentials. Here's what we decide:

Who's Coming

We've had as many as thirteen hunters in our camp and as few as four. While the core of the camp consists of individuals with some connection to the Ballard name, some friends usually come along as well. Over the years, a number of folks have frequented the camp often enough to be viewed as regulars. Others have popped in for a single season and never returned.

Most of the time the camp has been large enough to accommodate pretty much everyone who has wanted to come. By unspoken rule, however, if there are more hands in the air than places in camp, relatives take priority over the friends of individual camp members. And hunters with a history at camp trump newcomers.

If you were to survey our potential wall-tent population in midsummer, you'd swear that there's no way an encampment even twice the size of our normal setup would accommodate all the hunters. But from July to September, a curious population-control mechanism kicks in. Reluctant spouses, strong-willed employers, diesel-pickup payments, and a host of other human affairs quickly shrink the count. In early September last season I thought that we might have ten or twelve hunters in camp. Five actually showed.

Perhaps the best move is setting a deadline for "making up your mind." How can the cook plan meals and buy food when the maybes outnumber the committed? How can the wrangler stock weed-free hay and anticipate the number of pack animals when the actual number of riders and hunters is still a mystery?

Depending on the circumstances, we require people to give a definitive *yes* anywhere from two to four weeks before the camp—the more folks who might be camping, the longer the required lead time. Hunters who commit are expected to front a specific dollar amount to facilitate the purchase of food, fuel, hay, and other necessary items. This not only funds those doing the actual buying, but tends to discourage people from backing out at the last minute. Once you've paid your "up front" money, those attending the camp are under no obligation to return this deposit if you back out.

Hunters who don't spend the whole time in camp are another matter worth discussing. Some of my relatives feel strongly that if you can't commit for the full week, or more, you shouldn't come at all. These are middle-aged men with good jobs that allow ample paid vacation for a week's elk hunting.

I actually don't mind if someone can only swing a four-day weekend away from work. However, that goes with two expectations. First, the individuals who head home early pay the same amount as everyone else. Second, they pitch in doubly with chores while present as they won't be there to help with the hard work of breaking camp.

Who Pays for What

Some costs, such as food, are easy to figure and divide among the hunters, but things like gas for vehicles are a little more problematic. Then there are long-term expenses related to the maintenance of tents and other camping gear that may only show up in years when a tent needs to be replaced or repaired or a new piece of gear purchased.

Calculating expenses fairly also depends on who owns the gear. As it evolved, our camp came to hold all the basic items—tents, heating and cooking stoves, dishes, lanterns, etc.—in common. These things were stored in a shed on my folks' ranch. I've also shared elk camps where several parties pitched in with whatever items they could offer in service of the expedition.

So how do you weight these factors and figure out what individuals should pay? The important thing is to communicate with one another up front regarding expectations. In my extended hunting family, each

CAMP COSTS

While we're on the subject of expenses, let's look at what it costs to acquire and maintain a serviceable elk camp. Suppose five like-minded fellows get together to start a camp. How would they estimate the costs? Here's one example:

One 12 x 14 cook tent with 5-foot sidewalls $625
One internal frame for 12 x 14 tent $450
One 14 x 17 sleeping tent with 5-foot sidewalls $725
One internal frame for 14 x 17 tent $580
Heavy-duty floors for both tents $330
Heavy-duty flies for both tents. $450
Two high-quality woodburning stoves, pipe. $500
One heavy-duty, two-burner cookstove $160
Lanterns, cookware, table, miscellaneous gear $300

Total $4,120

I estimated the above figures on the high side, so the initial investment for each hunter in camp is about $800. Keep in mind, though, that this is a first-class camp. There are a number of ways to reduce startup costs.

The first year, the group could get by with just the two tents, wood stoves, cookstove, lanterns, and other gear. A couple of utility tarps could serve for rain flies on both tents and the tents could be pitched with wood poles instead of internal frames. This drops the initial investment to less than $500 per person. If that's still too much, they could put off purchasing the cook tent and its wood stove for a year. That brings the price per person down to around $300.

Each member of the group might then set aside $25 per month toward the elk camp, annually adding an extra $1,500 to acquire additional gear. In just a few years, the outfit would own a superb camp that would adequately service the owners and a few friends for decades to come—with proper care, of course.

How much you spend on your elk camp all depends on how elaborate you make it. But don't skimp on essentials.

person who purchases items specifically for camp keeps the receipts. Gas for vehicles transporting livestock, gear, and hunters from a prearranged meeting point to the camp is recorded as well. And an extra fee of about 10 percent of the actual expense is added to each hunter's bill for maintenance and equipment replacement.

A semi-trustworthy cousin keeps the reserve funds in a savings account until they need to be spent. The system works very well, because even folks who only unroll their sleeping bags in our tents for a single fall still pitch in a little for the maintenance of the camp.

Excluding gear purchases, how much does it cost to spend a week hunting at an established elk camp? Actually, it's much cheaper than you—or your spouse—might think. Last season, five of us enjoyed a week in the family camp. After meeting at the ranch to load gear, we drove two pickups, one pulling a horse trailer, ninety miles to the campsite. Collecting $110 per person provided for an excellent menu including salmon, baked ham, pot roast, traditional breakfasts, and more snacks and desserts than one ought to consume in a year. The cost also included gas for the pickups and feed for a pack mule—all for a whopping $22 per person, per day.

The Workload

A lot of work goes into the elk-camp experience, but I enjoy every aspect (except washing dishes). That said, I still expect other members of the camp to pitch in and shoulder their share of the load.

When I first started attending camp, my dad and two uncles had clearly defined roles. Uncle Jack was the wrangler. His primary responsibilities included keeping the horses fed and watered, maintaining tack, and hoping someone brought a "bronc" to the mountains so he could display his riding skills. As the road to our camp is impassable with horse trailers, Jack also drew the sometimes miserable job of riding seven miles to bring the stock in from what served as the main road. Although not an official duty, his storytelling—recounting in colorful detail the previous years' escapades—seemed an additional part of his job description.

Uncle Tom was the engineer. Lanterns that sputtered, fussy chainsaws, gunsmithing jobs, and any other task that required mechanical ingenuity fell to Tom. For many years, he and a few other fellows took the camp in and set it up a week before the season opened. Tom would then pass a peaceful sojourn by himself in the high country, kicking back and making sure everything was in working order before the rest of the hunters arrived.

My dad did the cooking. He wasn't grouchy all the time, but he sure got that way at elk camp. It was, I think, something of a game.

A good cook in a camp full of hungry men can get away with a lot of antisocial behavior as long as he keeps the grub coming. Dad liked to see how far he could push the envelope.

Under the leadership of the three brothers, a host of other camp chores were accomplished. A stack of firewood was cut and heaped outside each tent. At nightfall, enough wood was brought inside to keep the stoves burning through the dark hours. Lanterns were fueled each evening. Dishes were washed and put away after every meal. Once the camp was pitched the workload wasn't toilsome, but everyone was expected to contribute some labor. Some of my first camp chores involved subduing a pile of dirty dishes and fetching firewood.

Occasionally we've had a fellow in camp who didn't quite understand the concept of helping out. One gentleman, a friend's father-in-law, evidently felt he was above menial camp chores and seemed to disappear whenever work needed to be done. After dinner one evening, a cousin of mine dropped a dishcloth on his plate before he could escape from the cook tent. He took the hint and did the dishes—once.

The best way to ensure that everyone has a stake in the camp chores is to communicate that expectation. One of the most satisfying aspects of our family's camp is the transmission of outdoor skills from one generation to the next. Observing and assisting with pitching the wall tents taught me how to build a pole frame and erect a tent. Helping with meat-packing chores allowed me to acquire the skills to halve an elk to be carried on a riding saddle or quarter it for the panniers of a packsaddle.

Because I was expected to help out with these tasks as a youth, I'm now able to pass along that knowledge to others.

Behavioral Standards

Like politics, different standards of behavior can strain relations at elk camp. There's no need to post a list of rules on every tent flap and hitching rail, but it's wise to inform newcomers of the behavioral code of the camp. Men seem especially willing to let their hair down, even if they don't actually have any. Fellows who religiously avoid alcohol the rest of the year may take a nip to celebrate an elk kill—or for no reason at all. Does your camp have any expectations regarding the consumption of alcohol? If so, communicate them to visitors.

Smoking is another potentially contentious behavior. Whether or not you have a cigar or cigarette isn't really anyone else's business. However, smoking inside a tent might be a major annoyance to others. Discuss such matters beforehand so they won't cause problems.

Happily mixing personalities at elk camp is quite simple. If you take into account the wishes of others and remember that they're only sharing space with you for a week or so a year, the memories made hunting together will be good ones.

THE ROCKY MOUNTAIN
ELK FOUNDATION

The Elk Foundation is an international, nonprofit wildlife habitat conservation organization. With more than 150,000 members, the Elk Foundation has protected and enhanced more than 4.3 million acres of wildlife habitat throughout North America. Founded in 1984, the Elk Foundation is headquartered in Missoula, Montana, with its Canadian headquarters in Rocky Mountain House, Alberta.

The Elk Foundation is represented in all fifty states, plus an international membership in Canada and twenty-six foreign countries. The Elk Foundation's notable success stems largely from its dedicated and enthusiastic membership. The commitment to wildlife conservation and love of America's rich wildlife legacy are at the heart of what the founders of the Elk Foundation glimpsed upon establishing the organization.

The Elk Foundation meets its mission by funding the following types of efforts:

- Habitat enhancement projects such as prescribed burns, noxious weed treatments, and water developments;
- Wildlife management projects such as elk transplants and population monitoring;
- Research on elk and their habitat to provide wildlife managers with information needed to manage elk;
- Conservation education programs to increase public awareness of the importance of wildlife and their habitat;
- Land protection projects such as acquisitions and conservation easements; and

• Hunting heritage projects to promote ethical hunting and ensure future hunting opportunities.

Contact:
The Rocky Mountain Elk Foundation
5705 Grant Creek Road
P.O. Box 8249
Missoula, MT 59807
1-800-CALL ELK (1-800-225-5355)
1-406-523-4500
1-406-523-4550 (fax)
info@rmef.org
www.rmef.org

SELECT BIBLIOGRAPHY

Curtis, Sam. *The Complete Book of Elk Hunting: Tips and Tactics for All Weather and Habitat Conditions* (Rocky Mountain Elk Foundation Book). Guilford, CT: The Lyons Press. 2005.

Elk Hunting Secrets. (By members of the Rocky Mountain Elk Foundation). Guilford, CT: Falcon Press. 1999.

Robb, Bob. *The Ultimate Guide to Elk Hunting.* Guilford, CT: The Lyons Press. 2001.

Zumbo, Jim. *Elk Hunter's Bible.* Accokeek, MD: Stoeger Publishing. 2003.

RESOURCE GUIDE

The best products and information for creating a first-class elk camp aren't always available locally, so check out the sources below. A few of these companies don't sell directly to the consumer, but their Web sites have links to mail-order retailers.

Bass Pro Shops. Wall tents, sleeping bags, good military-style sleeping cots, pads, stoves, and numerous other items great for elk camps; 1-800-227-7776 or www.basspro.com.

Cabela's. The giant outdoor retailer sells wall tents, frames, stoves, cots, some horsepacking supplies, and other elk-camp goodies; 1-800-237-4444 or www.cabelas.com.

Camp Chef. Look to Camp Chef for great cooking products such as top quality stove/cookers, griddles, grill boxes, and accessories; 1-800-650-2433 or www.campchef.com.

Campmor. Mail-order retailer replete with camping supplies, including some hard-to-find and specialty items; 1-800-525-4784 or www.campmor.com.

Centers for Disease Control. A comprehensive government source for information pertaining to water purification and the prevention of parasitic infection; www.cdc.gov.

Coleman. For decades Coleman has been a leader in products for outdoor recreation. They have an excellent line of lanterns (check out the bright tube-type models), sleeping bags, stoves, cookware, cots, portable hot-water units, and other products. Backcountry users will find fine products at value prices in their Exponent line; 1-800-835-3278 or www.coleman.com.

Cylinder Stoves. Known for their quality steel wood stoves, this company also sells wall tents, frames, and related products; 1-800-586-3829 or www.cylinderstoves.com.

Kni-Co. A maker of fine sheet-metal stoves, Kni-Co also sells wall tents and frames; 541-886-8055 or www.kni-co.com.

Kwik Kamp. This company produces excellent joint kits for creating your own internal wall-tent frame. They also sell wall tents, frames, and stoves, including a high-tech titanium stove that weighs just over ten pounds; 541-558-3960 or www.kwikkamp.com.

L.L. Bean. Quality products have been the double-L hallmark for decades. Their fine sleeping bags and related products are an excellent addition to any elk camp; 1-800-441-5713 or www.llbean.com.

Montana Canvas. One of the country's leading manufacturers of wall tents, frames, and related items. Check out their line of lightweight wall tents for backcountry camps. Their Web site contains useful information about wall-tent camping along with profiles of their products; 1-800-235-6518 or www.montanacanvas.com.

Outfitter's Supply. Carries a complete line of horsepacking supplies, saddles, portable electric fence units, wall tents, and stoves. Also look at the handy question-and-answer resource guide to horsepacking on their Web site; 1-888-467-2256 or www.outfitterssupply.com.

REI. REI is well-known among backpackers and climbers for their backcountry gear. An excellent source for water purifiers, sleeping bags and pads, lightweight stoves, and other weight-wise products. Their Web site also has useful tips on water purification and other backcountry skills; 1-800-426-4840 or www.rei.com.

U.S. Forest Service. Search their Web site for useful information on camping in bear country or follow links to helpful regional resources; www.fs.fed.us.

INDEX

ABOUT THE AUTHOR

For nearly thirty years, a wall tent in Montana's Snowcrest Mountains has been Jack Ballard's favorite home away from home. A third-generation Montana native of homesteader's stock, Jack grew up on a ranch west of Three Forks, hunting mule deer, antelope, and elk.

In 1992 his first published photo appeared in the Rocky Mountain Elk Foundation's fledgling *Bugle* magazine. The next year, *Rocky Mountain Game & Fish* magazine carried his first article. Since then, Jack's articles and photos have appeared in over thirty regional and national magazines, including *American Hunter, Petersen's Hunting, Sports Afield, Northwest Fly Fishing, Colorado Outdoors, Deer & Deer Hunting,* and *Montana* magazine. His photos have been published in numerous books—including titles from the Smithsonian Press and the Heinemann Library—calendars, and magazines. Jack has received multiple awards for his writing and photography from the Outdoor Writers Association of America and other professional organizations.

While developing his writing career, Jack lectured in philosophy, religion, ethics, and education at Montana State University–Billings. He holds two master's degrees and is an accomplished public speaker, entertaining students, conference attendees, and recreation/conservation groups with his compelling narratives.

In addition to western big-game hunting, Jack also writes about fishing, camping, canoeing, cross-country skiing, wildlife, and conservation. When not wandering the backcountry, he hangs his hat in Billings, Montana.

To see more of Jack's work, visit www.jackballard.com. Contact him directly by e-mail: jackballard@earthlink.net.